LOVE LETTERS
TO THE
UNIVERSE

LOVE LETTERS
TO THE
UNIVERSE

QUOTATIONS **FOR** INDEPENDENT THINKERS

BY RICHARD KEHL

LOVE LETTERS
TO THE
UNIVERSE

...the heron, unseen for weeks, came flying widewinged toward me, settled just offshore on his post, took up his vigil. If you ask why this cleared a fog from my spirit, I have no answer.

DENISE LEVERTOV

Somewhere, there is something incredible waiting to be known.

CARL SAGAN

To the Universe, stars and planets are minor impurities.

ANONYMOUS ASTRONOMER

It was a morning in early summer. A silver haze shimmered and trembled over the lime trees. The air was laden with their fragrance. The temperature was like a caress. I remember – I need not recall – that I climbed up a tree stump and felt suddenly immersed in It-ness. I did not call it by that name. I had no need for words. It and I were one.

BERNARD BERENSON

I see nothing but infinities on all sides which surround me as an atom, and as a shadow which endures only for an instant and is no more.

BLAISE PASCAL

A slight sound at evening lifts me up by the ears, and makes life seem inexpressibly serene and grand. It may be in Uranus, or it may be in the shutter.

HENRY DAVID THOREAU

A single neuron may be rather dumb, but it is dumb in many subtle ways.

FRANCIS CRICK

You do not have to sit outside in the dark. If, however, you want to look at the stars, you will find that darkness is necessary. But the stars neither require nor demand it.

ANNIE DILLARD

If you don't become the ocean you'll be seasick every day.

LEONARD COHEN

You see, one thing is, I can live with doubt and uncertainty and not knowing. I think it's much more interesting to live not knowing than to have answers which might be wrong. I have approximate answers and possible beliefs and different degrees of certainty about different things, but I'm not absolutely sure of anything and there are many things I don't know anything about, such as whether it means anything to ask why we're here, and what the question might mean. I might think about it a little bit and if I can't figure it out, then I go on to something else, but I don't have to know an answer. I don't feel frightened by not knowing things, by being lost in a mysterious universe without having any purpose, which is the way it really is so far as I can tell. It doesn't frighten me.

    RICHARD FEYNMAN

On the whole, love comes with the speed of light, separation, with that of sound.

    JOSEPH BRODSKY

Why should the universe be constructed in such a way that atoms acquire the ability to be curious about themselves?

    MARCUS CHOWN

I can imagine no terminal point of human inquiry into nature, ever.

    LEWIS THOMAS

Space and time … are names.

    SIDDHA NAGARJUNA

Everything is unique, nothing happens more than once in a lifetime. The physical pleasure which a certain woman gave you at a certain moment, the exquisite dish which you ate on a certain day – you will never meet either again. Nothing is repeated, and everything is unparalleled.

    THE GONCOURT BROTHERS

Once the entire world is yourself, what could a life of solitude add?

    MAHADEVIYAKKA

When I was frustrated trying to understand gravity as the curvature of spacetime, he told me he often felt the same way. He told the story of the peasant who asks the engineer how a steam engine works. The engineer gives a detailed explanation, drawing diagrams, showing where the fuel goes in, how heat is transformed into motion and so forth. When the engineer is done, the peasant says he understands perfectly. Just one more question: "Where is the horse?"

K.C. COLE AND VICTOR WEISSKOPF

The breeze at dawn has secrets to tell you. Don't go back to sleep. You must ask for what you really want. Don't go back to sleep. People are going back and forth across the doorsill where the two worlds touch. The door is round and open. Don't go back to sleep.

RUMI

One could entertain the idea that the real world requires more than one, or possibly all, of the theories permitted by the mathematics.

M.P. BLENCOWE AND MICHAEL DUFF

Reminder: What am I doing on a level of consciousness where this is real?

SOURCE UNKNOWN

Within our bodies course the same elements that flame in the stars.

SUSAN SCHIEFELBEIN

"If any of them can explain it," said Alice, "I'll give him sixpence. I don't believe there's an atom of meaning in it." "If there's no meaning in it," said the King, "that saves a world of trouble, you know, as we needn't try to find any."

LEWIS CARROLL

I put it around my neck … it became a string of lovely pearls, each with a moon inside. My room then was full of moonlight as if the full moon had found its way in through the open window.

MIRABAI

Only in us is Go d so lost that He asks questions.

ST. TERESA OF AVILA

Imagine the fifteenbillionyear lifetime of the universe compressed into the span of a single year ... Dinosaurs emerge on Christmas Eve; flowers arise on December 28th; and men and women originate at 10:30 pm on New Year's Eve. All of recorded history occupies the last ten seconds of December 31.

CARL SAGAN

Wherever you are is the entry point.

KABIR

...then his heart is nothing but light, his subtle body is light, his material covering is light, his hearing, his sight, his hand, his exterior, his interior, are nothing but light.

NAJM RAZI

I believe a blade of grass is no less than the journeywork of the stars.

WALT WHITMAN

I had never comprehended this, the absoluteness of never.

JOHN FOWLES

The universe is made up of stories, not atoms.

MURIEL RUCKEYSER

Students achieving oneness will move ahead to twoness.

WOODY ALLEN

The ancient question is still awaiting an answer: What features in our brain account for our humanity, our musical creativity, infinitely varied artifacts, subtlety of humor, sophisticated projection (in chess, politics, and business), our poetry, ecstasy, fervor, contorted morality, and elaborate rationalization?

THEODORE H. BULLOCK

Sometimes I go about in pity for myself, and all the while a great wind is bearing me across the sky.

OJIBWA SAYING

Believe me, nothing moves me so deeply as the incredible, unprecedented miraculousness of my existence, which from the beginning followed such an impossible plot and yet has progressed from deliverance to deliverance.

RAINER MARIA RILKE

Everything existing in the Universe is the fruit of chance and necessity.

DEMOCRITOS

How it is that anything so remarkable as a state of consciousness comes about as a result of irritating nervous tissue, is just as unaccountable as the appearance of the Djin, when Aladdin rubbed his lamp.

ALDOUS HUXLEY

Having seen a small part of life, swift to die, men rise and fly away like smoke, persuaded only of what each has met with ... Who then claims to find the whole?

EMPEDOCLES

The experimentally known fact that all the elementary particles can be transformed into one another is an indication that it could scarcely be possible to single out one particular group of such particles ... One finds structures (in the theory of elementary particles) so linked and entangled with each other that it is really impossible to make further changes at any point without calling all the connections into question.

WERNER HEISENBERG

There are only two ways to live your life: as though nothing is a miracle, or as though everything is a miracle.

ALBERT EINSTEIN

What is the ultimate truth about ourselves? Various answers suggest themselves. We are a bit of stellar matter gone wrong. We are physical machinery – puppets that strut and talk and laugh and die as the hand of time pulls the strings beneath. But there is one elementary inescapable answer. We are that which asks the question.

SIR ARTHUR EDDINGTON

If we wish to understand the nature of the Universe we have an inner hidden advantage: we are ourselves little portions of the universe and so carry the answer within us.

JACQUES BOIVIN

The world began with what it is now the fashion to call "the Big Bang" ... it could not, of course, with no atmosphere to conduct waves of sound, and no ears. It was something else, occurring in the most absolute silence we can imagine. It was the Great Light.

LEWIS THOMAS

We are the transformers of the earth; our entire existence, the flights and plunges of our lOve, everything qualifies us for this task.

RAINER MARIA RILKE

Man is a microcosm, or a little world, because he is an extract from all the stars and planets of the whole firmament, from the earth and the elements; and so he is their quintessence.

THEOPHRASTUS PARACELSUS

For you, the world is weird because if you're not bored with it you're at odds with it. For me the world is weird because it is stupendous, awesome, mysterious, unfathomable; my interest has been to convince you that you must assume responsibility for being here in this marvelous time. I wanted to convince you that you must learn to make every act count, since you are going to be here for only a short while, in fact, too short for witnessing all the marvels of it.

CARLOS CASTANEDA

On the one hand, our image of reality is more than physical reality in that it contains many qualities not present in physical reality. Consider our experience of the color green, for example. In the physical world there is light of various frequencies, but the light itself is not green, nor are the electrical impulses that are transmitted from the eye to the brain. No color exists there. The green we see is a quality created in consciousness. It exists only as a subjective experience in the mind.

PETER RUSSELL

At times I think and at times I am.

PAUL VALERY

The airy sky has taken its place leaning against the wall. It is like a prayer to what is empty. And what is empty turns its face to us and whispers: "I am not empty, I am open."

TOMAS TRANSTROMER

I believe there are 15 747 436 275 002 577 605 653 961 181 555 468 044 717 914 527 116 709 366 231 425 076 185 631 031 296 296 protons in the universe and the same number of electrons.

SIR ARTHUR EDDINGTON

Throughout my whole life, during every minute of it, the world has been gradually lighting up and blazing before my eyes until it has come to surround me, entirely lit up from within.

PIERRE TEILHARD DE CHARDIN

Start seeing everything as God, but keep it a secret.

HAFIZ

I have done a terrible thing: I have postulated a particle that cannot be detected.

WOLFGANG PAULI (AFTER POSTULATING THE EX-
ISTENCE OF THE NEUTRINO)

Every part of this earth is sacred to my people. Every shining pine needle, every sandy shore, every mist in the dark woods, every clearing and humming insect is holy in the memory and experience of my people. The sap which courses through the trees carries the memories of the red man.

CHIEF SEATTLE

If a piece of popcorn were dropped on a neutron star, it would produce as much energy as a World War II atomic bomb.

NEIL MCALEER

There is a crack in everything. That's how the light gets in.

LEONARD COHEN

I can safely say that nobody understands quantum mechanics … Do not keep saying to yourself … "But how can it be like that?" because you will get "down the drain," into a blind alley from which nobody has yet escaped. Nobody knows how it can be like that.

RICHARD FEYNMAN

There is a lake so tiny that a mustard seed would cover it easily, yet everyone drinks from this lake. Deer, jackals, rhinoceroses, and sea elephants keep falling into it, falling and dissolving almost before they have time to be born.

LALLA

Who cares about half a second after the big bang: what about the half a second before?

FAY WELDON

No, what raised eyebrows was the fact that the astronomers only figured in the color of the universe as it would seem to human eyes – an awfully anthropocentric way to look at things: me, me, me. The universe would look quite different to a snake or a cat or a bee or a bat.

K.C. COLE

Pull the bow: a gentle motion. God will do the rest.

WILLIAM STAFFORD

Our brains evolved so that we could survive out there in the jungle. Why in the world should a brain develop for the purpose of being at all good at grasping the true underlying nature of reality?

BRIAN GREENE

O dark, dark, dark. They all go into the dark. The vacant interstellar spaces, the vacant into the vacant.

T.S. ELIOT

What do they call it … the primordial soup? The glop? That heartbreaking second when it all got together, the sugars and the acids and the ultraviolets, and the next thing you knew there were tangerines and string quartets.

EDWARD ALBEE

You have been invited to meet The Friend. No one can resist a Divine Invitation. That narrows down all our choices to just two: We can come to God Dressed for Dancing, or be carried on a stretcher to God's ward.

HAFIZ

Ideas are to objects as constellations are to stars.

WALTER BENJAMIN

This – the immediate, everyday, and present experience – is IT, the entire and ultimate point for the existence of a universe.

ALAN WATTS

Matter has reached the point of beginning to know itself ... a star's way of knowing about stars.

GEORGE WALD

If I had my life to live over again, I would start barefoot earlier in the spring.

85 YEAR OLD WOMAN

Sometimes I have a terrible need of, shall I say the word, religion. Then I go out at night and paint the stars.

VINCENT VAN GOGH

So what is this mind; what are these atoms with consciousness? Last week's potatoes! That is how I can remember what was going on in my mind a year ago – a mind which has long ago been replaced. That is what it means when one discovers how long it takes for the atoms of the brain to be replaced by other atoms, to note that the thing which I call my individuality is only a pattern or dance. The atoms come into my brain, dance a dance, then go out: always new atoms but always doing the same dance, remembering what the dance was yesterday.

RICHARD FEYNMAN

Imagine the time the particle you are returns where it came from!

RUMI

Everything around us is filled with mystery and magic. I find this no cause for despair, no reason to turn for solace to esoteric formulae or chariots of gods. On the contrary, our inability to find easy answers fills me with a fierce pride in our ambivalent biology ... with a constant sense of wonder and delight that we should be part of anything so profound.

LYALL WATSON

Everything speaks: the flowing airstream and the sailing halcyon, the blade of grass, the flower, the bud, the element; did you imagine the universe to be otherwise?

VICTOR HUGO

I walked around as you do, investigating the endless star. During the night, I woke up naked and the only thing caught in my net – a fish trapped inside the wind.

PABLO NERUDA

We inhale many hundreds of particles in each breath we take. Salt crystals from ocean whitecaps, dust scraped off distant mountains, micro bits of cooled magma blown from volcanoes and charred microfragments from tropical forest fires.

DAVID BODANIS

We die containing a richness of lovers and tribes, tastes we have swallowed, bodies we have plunged into and swum up as if rivers of wisdom, characters we have climbed into as if trees, fears we have hidden in as if caves. I wish for all this to be marked on my body when I am dead. I believe in such cartography – to be marked by nature, not just to label ourselves on a map like the names of rich men and women on buildings. We are communal histories, communal books. We are not owned or monogamous in our taste or experience. All I desired was to walk upon such an earth that had no maps.

MICHAEL ONDAATJE

"I am your own way of looking at things," she said. "When you allow me to live with you, every glance at the world around you will be a sort of salvation." And I took her hand.

WILLIAM STAFFORD

No; we have been as usual asking the wrong question. It does not matter a hoot what the mockingbird on the chimney is singing … the real and proper question is: why is it beautiful?

ANNIE DILLARD

Clouds come from time to time – and bring a chance to rest from looking at the moon.

BASHO

But are we being dreamed by a single divine intelligence, by God, or are we being dreamed by the collective consciousness of all things – by all the electrons, Z particles, butterflies, neutron stars, sea cucumbers, human and nonhuman intelligences in the universe? We cannot ask if the part is creating the whole, or the whole is creating the part because the part is the whole. So whether we call the collective consciousness of all things "God," or simply "The consciousness of all things," it doesn't change the situation. The universe is sustained by an act of such stupendous and ineffable creativity that it simply cannot be reduced to such terms. Again it is a selfreference cosmology. Or as the Kalahari Bushmen so eloquently put it, "The dream is dreaming itself."

MICHAEL TALBOT

Why is thought, being a secretion of the brain, more wonderful than gravity, a property of matter?

CHARLES DARWIN

One thing I'd like to know most of all: when those ants have made the Hill, and are all there, touching and exchanging, and the whole mass begins to behave like a single huge creature, and thinks, what on earth is that thought? And while you're at it, I'd like to know a second thing: when it happens, does any single ant know about it? Does his hair stand on end?

LEWIS THOMAS

Who can say where the electron really travels? You watch it the way you watch a cat run behind a slat fence.

DIANE ACKERMAN

Time is the substance from which I am made. Time is a river which carries me along, but I am the river; it is a tiger that devours me, but I am the tiger; it is a fire that consumes me, but I am the fire.

JORGE LUIS BORGES

We are something we can't know.

MICHAEL EIGEN

No one can stand in these solitudes unmoved, and not feel that there is more in man than the mere breath of his body.

CHARLES DARWIN

A balance that does not tremble cannot weigh.

ERWIN CHARGAFF

The Navaho have that wonderful image of what they call the pollen path. Pollen is the life source. The pollen path is the path to the center. The Navaho say, "Oh, beauty before me, beauty behind me, beauty to the right of me, beauty to the left of me, beauty above me, beauty below me, I'm on the pollen path."

JOSEPH CAMPBELL

It would be wonderful to tag an atom of carbon, say, the way an ornithologist bands birds with some sort of tiny transmitter, so that we could track its journey. An atom of carbon is, as far as we know, a permanent thing (provided it is not the radioactive form of carbon known as carbon 14). Every carbon atom that ever was, still is. The carbon atoms of the Earth's crust were once, before the Earth was born, part of the dusty nebulas of space. A carbon atom on the surface of the Earth makes its way around and around like a pilgrim or a gypsy, now into a rock, now into the sea, now into the air, now into the body of a living creature.

CHET RAYMO

We have all come to the right place. We all sit in God's classroom. Now, the only thing left for us to do, my dear, is to stop throwing spitballs for a while.

HAFIZ

Who would believe that so small a space could contain all the images of the universe?

LEONARDO DA VINCI, ON THE EYE

But the question remains: After physics has reduced the birth of the universe to an equation, is there room left for God? I posed this to a colleague who has done significant calculations on the origin of the universe and is also a devout believer in God. He answered that while physics can describe what is created, Creation itself lies outside physics. But with your equations, I said, you're not giving God any freedom. And he answered, "But that's his choice."

ALAN LIGHTMAN

Black holes are where God divided by zero.

BILL WATTERSON

But because truly being here is so much; because everything here apparently needs us, this fleeting world, which in some strange way keeps calling to us. Us, the most fleeting of all. Once for each thing. Just once; no more. And we too, just once. And never again. But to have been this once, completely even if only once: to have been at one with the earth, seems beyond undoing.

RAINER MARIA RILKE

The heart that breaks open can contain the whole universe.

JOANNA MACEY

Whoever you are, no matter how lonely, the world offers itself to your imagination, calls to you like the wild geese, harsh and exciting – over and over announcing your place in the family of things.

MARY OLIVER

In the landscape of spring, there is neither better nor worse. The flowering branches grow naturally, some long, some short.

ZEN SAYING

I know noble accents and lucid, inescapable rhythms; but I know, too, that the blackbird is involved in what I know.

WALLACE STEVENS

When I had heard the learn'd astronomer, when the proofs, the figures, were ranged in columns before me, when I was shown the charts and diagrams, to divide, and measure them, when I sitting heard the astronomer where he lectured with much applause in the lectureroom, how soon unaccountable I became tired and sick, till rising and gliding out I wandered off by myself, in the mystical moist nightair, and from time to time looked up in perfect silence at the stars.

WALT WHITMAN

You do not belong to you. You belong to the Universe.

R. BUCKMINSTER FULLER

The physical body is acknowledged as dust, the personal drama as delusion. It is as if the world we perceive through our senses, that whole gorgeous and terrible pageant, were the breaththin surface of a bubble ... Both suffering and joy come then like a brief reflection, and death like a pin.

STEPHEN MITCHELL

When you drive down the road and the radio is blaring and the wind is blasting past the windows, the radio doesn't sound loud, because you move your zero. You're shifting zeros all the time.

THOMAS HUMPHREY

Doris Lessing began her fictional chronicle of space with this dedication: For my father, who used to sit, hour after hour, night after night, outside our home in Africa, watching the stars. "Well," he would say, "if we blow ourselves up, there's plenty more where we came from."

We do not see things as they are. We see them as we are.

THE TALMUD

I have seen sparks fly out when two stones are rubbed, so perhaps it is not dark inside after all ... Just enough light to make out the strange writings, the starcharts on the inner walls.

CHARLES SIMIC

Gravitation cannot be held responsible for people falling in love.

ALBERT EINSTEIN

Lord, you called to me, and I did only answer thee with words slow and sleepy: "Wait a while! Wait a little!" But while and while have no end, and wait a little is a long road.

ANONYMOUS 14TH CENTURY ENGLISH

The image on a television screen is produced by myriads of light pulses emitted when electrons fired from a gun at the back of the set strike the fluorescent screen. The picture you perceive is reasonably sharp because the number of electrons involved is enormous, and by the law of averages, the cumulative effect of many electrons is predictable. However, any particular electron, with its inbuilt unpredictability, could go anywhere on the screen. The arrival of this electron at a place, and the fragment of picture that it produces is uncertain. According to Bohr's philosophy bullets from an ordinary gun follow a precise path to their target, but electrons from an electron gun simply turn up at the target. And however good your aim, no bull'seye is guaranteed. The event "electron at place X on the television screen" cannot be considered as caused by the gun, or anything else. For there is no known reason why the electron should go to point X rather than some other place. The picture fragment is an event without a cause, an astonishing claim to remember when you next watch your favorite program.

SOURCE UNKNOWN

There is one common flow, one common breathing. All things are in sympathy.

HIPPOCRATES

The silence lives in the grass on the underside of every blade and in the blue spaces between the stones.

ROLF JACOBSEN

For the rest of my life I want to reflect on what light is.

ALBERT EINSTEIN

Look again at that dot. That's here. That's home. That's us. On it everyone you love, everyone you know, everyone you ever heard of, every human being who ever was, lived out their lives. The aggregate of our joy and suffering, thousands of confident religions, ideologies, and economic doctrines, every hunter and forager, every hero and coward, every creator and destroyer of civilization, every king and peasant, every young couple in love, every mother and father, hopeful child, inventor and explorer, every teacher of morals, every corrupt politician, every "superstar", every "supreme leader," every saint and sinner in the history of our species lived there – on a mote of dust suspended in a sunbeam.

    CARL SAGAN

Beyond these are other suns, giving light and life to other systems, not a thousand, or two thousand merely, but multiplied without end, and ranged all around us, at immense distances from each other, attended by ten thousand times ten thousand worlds, all in rapid motion; yet calm, regular and harmonious – all space seems to be illuminated, and every particle of light a world … And yet all this vast assemblages of suns and worlds may bear no greater proportion to what lies beyond the utmost boundaries of human vision, than a drop of water to the ocean.

    ELIJAH H. BURRITT

Mathematics is the loom upon which God weaves the fabric of the universe.

    CLIFFORD A. PICKOVER

The acceleration of a flea is twenty times more powerful that that of a moon rocket reentering the earth's atmosphere.

    MARGARET ROTHSCHILD

Imagine … that you could take a glass full of water from the ocean, and by some means paint the molecules purple so that they could be identified if you found them again. Then toss your glass full of purple molecules back into the ocean and allow them to mix completely with all the waters of the globe. Then take a second glass full of water from the ocean and look for purple molecules. You would find about 200! There are 200 times as many molecules in a glass of water as there are glasses of water in the world!

    DR. WILLIAM F. KIEFFER

I am a man: little do I last and the night is enormous. But I look up: the stars write. Unknowing I understand: I too am written, and at this very moment someone spells me out.

OCTAVIO PAZ

God said to Abraham, "But for me, you would not be here." "I know that Lord," Abraham answered, "But were I not here there would be no one to think about you."

TRADITIONAL JEWISH TALE

Our true home is the present moment. To live in the present moment is a miracle. The miracle is not to walk on water. The miracle is to walk on the green Earth in the present moment.

THICH NHAT HANH

If an angel were to tell us something of his philosophies, I do believe some of his propositions would sound like 2 x 2=13.

GEORG CHRISTOPH LICHTENBERG

All we are is light made solid.

SOURCE UNKNOWN

A world of dew is a world of dew … and yet, and yet…

ISSA

The brain is a threepound mass you can hold in your hand that can conceive of a universe a hundredbillion lightyears across.

MARIAN DIAMOND

To breath, to see, feel, touch, taste, hear, smell, realize the world, widely, without judgment or repudiation: this was the first task – to allow the world in. To inhale all, to swallow all, to become the place observed. For no more reason than its recognition … for when we breathe, when we see, feel, touch, taste, hear the world, we alter its materiality profoundly. What was simply an emitted signal, the outcry of a thing to let us know it was there, becomes a quality in consciousness. The object is visible because its messages can be received, but the message itself is invisible; it is nowhere; or, rather, it is now in an inner space, not the space between our ears, but the space between what our ears hear.

WILLIAM GASS

When spring comes, the grass grows by itself.

YUNMEN

It is not how things are in the world that is mystical, but that it exists. We feel that even when all possible scientific questions have been answered, the problems of life (or existence) remain completely untouched. Of course there are then no questions left, and this itself is the answer. The solution of the riddle of life (or existence) in space and time lies outside space and time. What we cannot speak about we must pass over in silence.

LUDWIG WITTGENSTEIN

The longing for all that is tall like palm trees. The yearning for all that is long like rivers ... the lament for all that is purple like dusk ... the weeping of all that weeps because it is far away ... very far away.

CASSIANO RICARDO

So we are grasped by what we cannot grasp; it has its inner light, even from a distance – and changes us, even if we do not reach it, into something else, which, hardly sensing it, we already are; a gesture waves us on, answering our own wave ...

RAINER MARIA RILKE

Nature cannot be ordered about, except by obeying her.

FRANCIS BACON

But then I drew up the curtain and looked out of the window. Yes, there it still was, the old External World, still apparently quite unaware of its own nonexistence. I felt helpless, smallboyish before it: I couldn't poohpooh it away.

LOGAN PEARSALL SMITH

With my hand I gather this emptiness, imponderable night, starry families, a chorus quieter than silence, a sound of the moon, some secret, a triangle, a chalk trapezoid.

PABLO NERUDA

It has been said repeatedly that one can never, try as he will, get around to the front of the universe. Man is destined to see only its far side, to realize nature only in retreat.

LOREN EISELEY

Part of the intellectual equipment of an educated person, however his or her time is to be spent, ought to be a feel for the queerness of nature, the inexplicable thing, the side of life for which informed bewilderment will be the best way of getting through the day.

LEWIS THOMAS

Rumi says that a human being is a polished mirror that cannot help reflecting. What we love, we are. We become reflected light. The polishing is done by the intensity of our longings.

The renowned Professor Bignumska, lecturing on the future of the universe, had just stated that in about a billion years, according to her calculations, the earth would fall into the sun in a fiery death. In the back of the auditorium a tremulous voice piped up: "Excuse me, Professor, but hhhow long did you say it would be?" Professor Bignumska calmly replied, "About a billion years." A sigh of relief was heard. "Whew! For a minute there, I thought you'd said a million years.

SOURCE UNKNOWN

You cannot have first space and then things to put into it, any more than you can have first a grin and then a Cheshire cat to fit on to it.

ALFRED NORTH WHITEHEAD

Our imagination is stretched to the utmost, not, as in fiction, to imagine things which are not really there but just to comprehend those things which are there.

RICHARD FEYNMAN

Judge a moth by the beauty of its candle.

RUMI

When I say "I am", I do not mean a separate entity with a body as its nucleus. I mean the totality of being, the ocean of consciousness, the entire universe.

SRI NISARAADATTA MAHARAJ

I am a passenger on Spaceship Earth.

R. BUCKMINSTER FULLER

Poetry works on the very surface of the eye, that thin, unyielding wall of liquid between mind and world, where, somehow, mysteriously, the patterns formed by electrical storms assaulting the retina become things and the thoughts of things and the names of things and the relations supposed between things.

HOWARD NEMEROV

Still there are moments when one feels free from one's own identification with human limitations and inadequacies. At such moments, one imagines that one stands on some spot of a small planet, gazing in amazement at the cold yet profoundly moving beauty of the eternal, the unfathomable: life and death flow into one and there is neither evolution nor destiny; only being.

ALBERT EINSTEIN

Could I have been around when the cosmos was one second old, we could have seen only objects less than one lightsecond away, not as far as the moon now is.

DIETRICK E. THOMSEN

I have always imagined that Paradise will be a kind of library.

JORGE LUIS BORGES

The more I work, the more I see things differently, that is, everything gains in grandeur every day, becomes more and more unknown, more and more beautiful. The closer I come, the grander it is, the more remote it is.

ALBERTO GIACOMETTI

Chance is perhaps the pseudonym of God when He did not want to sign.

ANATOLE FRANCE

Naturalist Loren Eiseley tells of coming upon a spider in a forest, spinning the sticky spokes of the web that extend her senses out into the world. Just so, humans with their scientific sense have spun a web that reaches far beyond our ears and eyes. And like the spider, we lie "at the heart of it, listening." Yet Eiseley is even more impressed at what the spider cannot perceive. "Spider thoughts in a spider universe – sensitive to raindrop and moth flutter, nothing beyond ... What is it we are a part of that we do not see...?"

K.C. COLE

For every human on earth, there are 200 million insects.

NEWSPAPER

All know that the drop merges into the ocean but few know that the ocean merges into the drop.

KABIR

It does not at present look as though Nature had designed the Universe primarily for life; the normal stars and the normal nebula have nothing to do with life except making it impossible.

SIR JAMES JEANS

The universe would never bother to create two Shakespeares. That would only reveal limited creativity. The Ultimate Mystery from which all beings emerge prefers Ultimate Extravagance, each being ... unique, never to be repeated.

BRIAN SWIMME

In every deep breath there must be a few molecules that I have pushed out with the first cry after my birth.

ARNOLD BENZ

We stand before a mystery, and in tampering with the earth we tamper with a mystery. We are in deep ignorance.

JONATHAN SCHELL

I have a friend who likes to ask the following "science" question: How would you hold one hundred tons of water in thin air with no visible means of support? Answer: Build a cloud.

K.C. COLE

A shudder goes through the universe, even long after. Every star, clasping its meaning as it looks back, races outward where something quiet and far waits. Within, too, ever receding into its fractions, that first brutal sound nestles closer and closer toward the tiny dot of tomorrow. And here we are in the middle, holding it all together, not even shaking. Hard to believe.

WILLIAM STAFFORD

Eternity is very long, especially near the end.

WOODY ALLEN

If the stars should appear one night in a thousand years, how would men believe and adore.

RALPH WALDO EMERSON

Is it not shocking to know that … all the heavens including all the luminaries whose lights are measured to reach this earth after millions of years are said to be mere bubbles in the ocean of eternal Emptiness?

D.T. SUZUKI

At Big Sur lighthouse, perched on a distant promontory, a beacon flashes to warn ships away from the coast and sandbanks, its light zooming out to them at 186,000 miles per second. The searchlight of the sun takes about eight minutes to reach Earth. And the light we see from the North Star set sail in the days of Shakespeare. Just think how straight the path of light is. Pass sunlight through a prism, though, and the light bends. Because each ray bends a different amount, the colors separate into a band. Many things catch the light prismatically – fish scales, the motherofpearl inside a limpet shell, oil on a slippery road, a dragonfly's wings, opals, soap bubbles, peacock feathers, the grooves in gramophone records, metal that's lightly tarnished, the neck of a hummingbird, the wing case of beetles, spiders' webs smeared with dew.

DIANE ACKERMAN

I came to love you too late, Oh Beauty, so ancient and so new. Yes, I came to love you too late. What did I know? You were inside me, and I was out of my body and mind, looking for you. I drove like an ugly madman against the beautiful things and beings you made. You were in fact inside me, but I was not inside you.

ST. AUGUSTINE

Each thing implies the universe.

JORGE LUIS BORGES

Ever wondered what the speed of lightning would be if it didn't zigzag?

SOURCE UNKNOWN

Enter here, through the yellow eyes of the cat and the daffodil. Bring your dreams. Walk to the top. Your bones will be the landscape and your thoughts will be as gardens grow: silent, blooming in the dark, surviving the season called snow.

ROSLYN NELSON

We cannot catch the fleeting minute and put it alongside a later minute.

EDWARD MILNE

The contradiction so puzzling to the ordinary way of thinking comes from the fact that we have to use language to communicate our inner experience which in its very nature transcends linguistics.

D.T. SUZUKI

I am standing on the threshold about to enter a room. It is a complicated business. In the first place I must shove against an atmosphere pressing with a force of fourteen pounds on every square inch of my body. I must make sure of landing on a plank traveling at twenty miles a second round the sun – a fraction of a second too early or too late, the plank would be miles away. I must do this whilst hanging from a round planet, heading outward into space.

SIR ARTHUR STANLEY EDDINGTON

So long as you haven't experienced this: to die and so to grow, you are only a troubled guest on the dark earth.

JOHANN WOLFGANG VON GOETHE

After all, mind is such an odd predicament for matter to get into. I often marvel how something like hydrogen, the simplest atom, forged in some early chaos of the universe, could lead to us and the gorgeous fever we call consciousness. If a mind is just a few pounds of blood, dream, and electric, how does it manage to contemplate itself, worry about its soul, do timeandmotion studies, admire the shy hooves of a goat, know that it will die, enjoy all the grand and lesser mayhems of the heart? How do you begin with hydrogen and end up with prom dresses, jealousy, chamber music?

DIANE ACKERMAN

And beyond our galaxy are other galaxies, in the universe all told at least a hundred billion, each containing a hundred billion stars. Do these figures mean anything to you?

JOHN UPDIKE

The ultimate stuff of the universe is mind stuff.

SIR ARTHUR EDDINGTON

After chopping off all the arms that reached out to me; after boarding up all the windows and doors; after filling all the pits with poisoned rats; after building my house on the rock of a No inaccessible to flattery and fear; after cutting out my tongue and eating it; after hurling handfuls of silence and monosyllables of scorn at my love; after forgetting my name and the name of my birth place and the name of my race; after judging myself and sentencing myself to perpetual loneliness, I heard against the stones of my dungeon of syllogisms the humid, tender, insistent onset of spring.

OCTAVIO PAZ

The only offering you can make to God is your increasing awareness.

LALLA

"The stars are made of the same atoms as the earth." I usually pick one small topic like this to give a lecture on. Poets say science takes away from the beauty of the stars – mere globs of gas atoms. Nothing is "mere". I too can see the stars on a desert night, and feel them. But do I see less or more? The vastness of the heavens stretches my imagination – stuck on this carousel my little eye can catch onemillionyearold light. A vast pattern – of which I am a part – perhaps my stuff was belched from some forgotten star, as one is belching there. Or see them with the greater eye of Palomar, rushing all apart from some common starting point when they were perhaps all together. What is the pattern, or the meaning, or the why? It does not do harm to the mystery to know a little about it. For far more marvelous is the truth than any artists of the past imagined! Why do the poets of the present not speak of it? What men are poets who can speak of Jupiter if he were like a man, but if he is an immense spinning sphere of methane and ammonia must be silent?

    RICHARD FEYNMAN

Anywhere is the center of the world

    BLACK ELK

Opening up wide to the fullness of life, Cezanne felt himself to be the conduit where nature and humanity met – "The landscape thinks itself in me … I am its consciousness".

Although atoms are way more than 99.99% empty space, I have a real problem in walking through a wall.

    LEON LEDERMAN

It is a curious circumstance, that when we wish to obtain a sight of a very faint star, we can see it most distinctly by looking away from it, and when the eye is turned full upon it, it immediately disappears.

    DAVID BREWSTER

Perhaps, as the essayist Lewis Thomas has suggested, we are part of a grand symphony that includes the "Rhythm of insects, the long pulsing runs of birdsong, the descants of whales, and the modulated vibration of a million locusts in migration …" He proposes we do not fully appreciate the music because we are not the audience, but rather members of the orchestra.

    T.S. ELIOT

It's come to the edge, the interface between what can be known, and is never to be discovered because it is a mystery that transcends all human research. The source of life – what is it? No one knows. We don't even know what an atom is, whether it is a wave or a particle – it is both. We don't have any idea of what these things are. That's the reason we speak of the divine. There's a transcendent energy source. When the physicist observes subatomic particles, he's seeing a trace on a screen. These traces come and go, come and go, and we come and go, and all of life comes and goes. That energy is the informing energy of all things.

JOSEPH CAMPBELL

One regret, dear world, that I am determined not to have when I am lying on my deathbed is that I did not kiss you enough.

HAFIZ

On the tidal mud, just before sunset, dozens of starfishes were creeping. It was as though the mud were a sky and enormous, imperfect stars moved across it as slowly as the actual stars cross heaven. All at once they stopped, and as if they had simply increased their receptivity to gravity they sank down into it and lay still; and by the time pink of sunset broke across them they were as invisible as the true stars at daybreak.

GALWAY KINNELL

I know that nothing has ever been real without my beholding it. All becoming has needed me. My looking ripens things and they come toward me, to meet and be met.

RAINER MARIA RILKE

When I was young, I forgot to laugh. Later when I opened my eyes and saw reality I began to laugh and haven't stopped.

SØREN KIERKEGAARD

This moment, this being, is the thing. My life is all life in little. The moon, the planets, pass around my heart. The sun, now hidden by the round bulk of this earth, shines into me, and in me as well. The gods and the angels both good and bad are like the hairs of my own head, seemingly numberless, and growing from within. I people the cosmos from myself, it seems, yet what am I? A puff of dust, or a brief coughing spell, with emptiness and silence to follow.

ALEXANDER ELIOT

And this our life exempt from public haunt finds tongues in trees, books in the running brooks, sermons in stones, and good in every-thing. I would not change it.

WILLIAM SHAKESPEARE

Why is a light ray so fast and a whisper so slow?

SOURCE UNKNOWN

I remain oppressed by the thought that the venture into space is meaningless unless it coincides with a certain interior expansion, an evergrowing universe within, to correspond with the far flight of the galaxies our telescopes follow from without.

LOREN EISELEY

The heat of midnight tears will bring you to God.

MIRABAI

Over all the hilltops Silence. Among all the treetops you feel hardly a breath moving. The birds fall silent in the woods. Simply wait! Soon you too will be silent.

JOHANN WOLFGANG VON GOETHE

Whence this creation has arisen – perhaps it formed itself or per-haps it did not – the one who looks down on it, in the highest, only he knows – or perhaps he does not know.

THE RIGVEDA

My doctrine is to think the thought that is unthinkable, to practice the deed that is not performable, to speak the speech that is inexpress-ible, and to be trained in the discipline that is beyond discipline.

THE SUTRA IN FORTY-TWO SECTIONS

The crux is that the vast majority of the mass of the universe seems
to be missing.

WILLIAM J. BROAD

Won't you come into the garden? I would like my roses to see you.

RICHARD B. SHERIDAN

And the problem arises: what is left over if I subtract the fact that my
arm goes up from the fact that I raise my arm?

LUDWIG WITTGENSTEIN

The secondcentury gnostic Valentinius held that the world was ac-
cidentally created by a female Demiurge named Sophia.

The 1911, the little town of Nakhla in Egypt was the scene of one of
the most remarkable events in history: a chunk of rock fell from the
sky and killed a dog, the only known canine fatality caused by a
cosmic object. Improbably though this encounter was, its truly extraordinary nature was revealed only decades later, when scientists
found the culprit was not a common or garden meteorite, but a
piece of the planet Mars.

PAUL DAVIES

When the ocean comes to you as a lover, marry, at once, quickly,
for God's Sake!

RUMI

If there was a big bang the universe must have consisted of an infinite amount of energy concentrated in a single point. God knows
where that came from.

GERHARD STAHUHN

Our perceiving self is nowhere to be found within the worldpicture,
because it itself is the worldpicture.

ERWIN SCHRODINGER

For example, they can remember that large numbers of anything
are bound to create coincidences. To wit: It is certain that at least
250 of the 25 million people living in the United States will experience a oneinamillion coincidence every day – purely by chance.

SOURCE UNKNOWN

The world is given but once. Nothing is reflected. The original and the mirrorimage are identical. The world extended in time and space is but our representation. Experience does not give us the slightest clue of its being anything besides that.

ERWIN SCHRODINGER

I don't really like driving in snow. There's something about the motion of the falling snowflakes that hurts my eyes, throwing my sense of balance all to hell. It's like tumbling into a field of stars.

NEIL GAIMAN

All that we know is nothing, we are merely crammed wastepaper baskets, unless we are in touch with that which laughs at all our knowing.

D.H. LAWRENCE

Be ready to orbit his lamp like a moth giving in to the light, to live in the deer as she runs toward the hunter's call, in the partridge that swallows hot coals for the love of the moon, in the fish that, kept from the sea, happily dies. Like a bee trapped for life in the closing of the sweet flower, Mira has offered herself to her Lord. She says, the single Lotus will swallow you whole.

MIRABAI

Bread is more in love with you than you with it. It sits and waits for days. It knows you have no will. If you could fast, bread would jump into your lap as lovers do with each other. Be full with trusting …

RUMI

We are simply the dust of the universe, trying to understand itself.

CHARLES PELLEGRINO

Patience, patience … patience in the blue sky! Every atom of silence is the chance of a ripe fruit!

PAUL VALERY

Is the universe a great mechanism, a great computation, a great symmetry, a great accident or a great thought?

JOHN D. BARROW

Take your practiced powers and stretch them out until they span the chasm between two contradictions … For the god wants to know himself in you.

RAINER MARIA RILKE

One day I met a friend in a corridor of my college. We both carried large books: hers an anthology of Elizabethan poetry, mine a volume of the Smithsonian Star Catalog. "Oh! Stars!" she said, "How wonderful!" I opened my book. It was full of numbers. The coordinates and specifications of 96,000 stars, in a book the size of the New York City telephone directory. Right ascensions and declinations, proper motions, radial velocities, spectral types, visual and absolute magnitudes, distances in parsecs. My friend's bright expression faded. "Grief brought to numbers cannot be so fierce," she said, quoting John Donne.

CHET RAYMO

There is an ineffable mystery that underlies ourselves and the world. It is the darkness from which the light shines. When you recognize the integrity of the universe, and that death is as certain as birth, then you can relax and accept that this is the way it is. There is nothing else to do.

ALAN WATTS

Student, tell me, what is God? He is the breath inside the breath.

KABIR

It is a primitive form of thought that things either exist or do not exist.

SIR ARTHUR EDDINGTON

Nature is not mute. It eternally repeats the same notes which reach us from afar, muffled, with neither harmony nor melody. But we cannot do without melody … It is up to us to strike the chords, to write the score, to bring forth the symphony, to give the sounds a form that, without us, they do not have.

FRANCOIS JACOB

On a train through Siberia, Laurens van der Post looked out the window at the huge expanse of flat country and endless sky. "I thought I had never been to any place with so much sky and space around it," he writes ... and was especially startled by "the immense thunder clouds moving out of the dark towards the sleeping city resembling, in the spasmodic lightning, fabulous swans beating towards us on hissing wings of fire." As Van der Post watched the lightning from the train, the Russian friend accompanying him explained that they had a special word in his language for just that scene: Zarnitsa.

DIANE ACKERMAN

A tree growing out of the ground is as wonderful today as it ever was. It does not need to adopt new and startling methods.

ROBERT HENRI

Blobs, spots, specks, smudges, cracks, defects, mistakes, accidents, exceptions, and irregularities are the windows to other worlds.

BOB MILLER

From complexity comes the capacity for difference. A sphere is a sphere is a sphere but no two snowflakes are exactly alike. And snowflakes are constructed only of simple water, a molecule of merely three atoms – H_2O.

K.C. COLE

All such notions as causation, succession, atoms, primary elements ... are all figments of the imagination and manifestations of the mind.

BUDDHA

We (that indivisible divinity that operates in us) have dreamed the world. We have dreamed it as enduring, mysterious, visible, omnipresent in space and stable in time; but we have consented to tenuous and eternal intervals of illogicalness in its architecture that we might know it is false.

JORGE LUIS BORGES.

How can a neuron feel compassion?

DIANE ACKERMAN

The universe can be best pictured ... as consisting of pure thought.

SIR JAMES JEANS

It could be that the real universe ... is perhaps what has been start-ed by some disastrous experiment performed some twenty billion years ago by a postgraduate student in order to test the structure of a vacuum of another universe.

OBHANN RAFELSKI AND BERNDT MULLER

If, as I believe, the urge to make a kind of music is as much a char-acteristic of biology as our other fundamental functions, there ought to be an explanation for it. If there were to be sounds to represent this process, they would have the arrangement of the Brandenburg Concertos for my ear, but I am open to wonder whether the same events are recalled by the rhythms of insects, the long, pulsing runs of birdsong, the descants of whales, the modulated vibrations of a million locusts in migration, the tympani of gorilla breasts, termite heads, drumfish bladders.

LEWIS THOMAS

Take a pitcher full of water and set it down on the water – now it has water inside and water outside. We mustn't give it a name, lest silly people start talking again about the body and the soul. If you want the truth, I'll tell you the truth: listen to the secret sound, the real sound, which is inside you. The one no one talks of speaks the secret sound to himself, and he is the one who has made it all.

KABIR

Is it not stirring to understand how the world actually works – that white light is made of colors, that transparent air reflects light, that in so doing it discriminates among the waves, and that the sky is blue for the same reason that the sunset is red? It does no harm to the romance of the sunset to know a little bit about it.

CARL SAGAN

Apart from the known and the unknown, what else is there?

HAROLD PINTER

How much starlight at any one time falls on Earth? The light from all the stars equals about one fifteenth the light of the full Moon or one sixmillionth of the Sun's light. If the sum of all starlight could be concentrated in one object, it would equal a 100watt bulb seen from a distance of 613 feet – about the length of two football fields.

NEIL MCALEER

Forget distinctions. Leap into the boundless and make it your home!

CHUANG TZU

The universe looks less and less like a great machine and more and more like a great thought.

SIR JAMES JEANS

Did you know the RNA/DNA molecule can be found throughout space in many galaxies ... only everybody spells it differently?

JANE WAGNER

The happiness of the drop is to die in the river.

ALGHAZALI

Here arises a puzzle that has disturbed scientists of all periods. How is it possible that mathematics, a product of human thought that is independent of experience, fits so excellently the objects of physical reality? Can human reason without experience discover by pure thinking the properties of real things?

ALBERT EINSTEIN

To a mind that is still the whole universe surrenders.

CHUANG TZU

According to quantum mechanics ... any two electrons must necessarily be completely identical, and the same holds for any two protons and for any two particles whatever, of any one particular kind. This is not to say that there is no way of telling the particles apart: the statement is considerably stronger than that. If an electron in a person's brain were to be exchanged with an electron in a brick, then the state of the system would be exactly the same state as it was before, not merely indistinguishable from it!

ROGER PENROSE

The Japanese esthetic honors the asymmetrical, the natural, or the accidental: God is everywhere, and the crack in the cup is equal in value to the most exquisitely painted lotus flower.

SOURCE UNKNOWN

The ideal universe for us is one very much like the universe we inhabit. And I would guess that this is not really much of a coincidence.

CARL SAGAN

We owe our very existence to accidents. The air we breathe is a miracle made by ancient bacteria. A random mutation somewhere along the evolutionary line started the process of photosynthesis, which causes plants to breathe our oxygen. As a result of it, many plants died, poisoned by their own exhalations; those that lived created the sky.

K.C. COLE

The world? Moonlit drops shaken from the crane's bill.

DOGEN

All scientific knowledge that we have of this world, or will ever have, is as an island in the sea of mystery. We live in our partial knowledge as the Dutch live on polders claimed from the sea. We dike and fill. We dredge up soil from the bed of mystery and build ourselves room to grow ... Scratch the surface of knowledge and mystery bubbles up like a spring. And occasionally, at certain disquieting moments in history (Aristarchus, Galileo, Planck, Einstein), a tempest of mystery comes rolling in from the sea and overwhelms our efforts...

CHET RAYMO

Sometimes I think we're alone. Sometimes I think we're not. In either case, the thought is staggering.

BUCKMINSTER FULLER

When the moon sails out the sea covers the earth and the heart feels it is a little island in the infinite.

FEDERICO GARCIA LORCA.

Whether or not we are at peace is not determined by what we have or do in the material world. We have created our perception of the world. We have given it all the meaning and value it has for us. And we are free to see it differently.

PETER RUSSELL

All night I could not sleep because of the moonlight on my bed. I kept on hearing a voice calling: Out of Nowhere, Nothing answered "Yes."

ZI YE

Quantum theory provides us with a striking illustration of the fact that we can fully understand a connection though we can only speak of it in images and parables.

WERNER HEISENBERG

How to upgrade the properties of matter to account for mind, and to tell how from the dust and water of the earth, natural forces conjured a mental system capable of asking why it exists.

NIGEL SLATER

For the real amazement, if you want to be amazed, is the process. You start out as a single cell derived from the coupling of a sperm and an egg, this divides into two, then four, then eight, and so on, and at a certain stage there emerges a single cell which will have as all its progeny the human brain. The mere existence of that cell should be one of the great astonishments of the earth. People ought to be walking around all day, all through their waking hours, calling to each other in endless wonderment, talking of nothing but that cell. If you like being surprised, there's the source. One cell is switched on to become the whole trillioncell, massive apparatus for thinking and imagining and, for that matter, being surprised. All the information needed for learning to read and write, playing the piano, arguing before senatorial subcommittees, walking across the street through traffic, or the marvelous human act of putting out one hand and leaning against a tree, is contained in that first cell. All of grammar, all syntax, all arithmetic, all music.

LEWIS THOMAS

Philosophers are always saying, "Well, just take a chair, for example." The moment they say that, you know that they do not know what they are talking about any more. What is a chair? Well, a chair is a certain thing over there .. certain? how certain? The atoms are evaporating from it from time to time – not many atoms, but a few – dirt falls on it and gets dissolved in the paint; so to define a chair precisely, to say exactly which atoms are chair, and which atoms are air, or which atoms are dirt, or which atoms are paint that belongs to the chair is impossible.

RICHARD FEYNMAN

Be humble for you are made of dung. Be noble for you are made of stars.

SERBIAN PROVERB

What you don't know determines what you think you know, in ways that aren't completely known to you.

HOWARD REINGOLD

And what he saw with his eyes was not even the real heavens. No, only white marks, bright vibrations, clouds of sky roe, tokens of the real thing, only as much as could be taken in through the distortions of the atmosphere. Through these distortions you saw objects, forms, partial realities. The rest was to be felt. And it wasn't only that you felt, but that you were drawn to feel and to penetrate further, as if you were being informed that what was spread over you had to do with your existence, down to the very blood and the crystal forms inside your bones. Rocks, trees, animals, men and women, these also drew you to penetrate further, under the distortions (comparable to the atmospheric ones, shadows within shadows), to find their real being with your own.

SAUL BELLOW

One instant is eternity; eternity is in the now. When you see through this one instant, you see through the one who sees.

WUMEN

Who would have dreamed that a tube connecting two lenses of glass would pierce the swarming depths of our being, force upon us incredible feats of sanitary engineering, master the plague, and create that giant upsurge out of unloosened human nature that we call the population explosion?

ARTHUR C. CLARKE

The heaventree of stars hung with humid nightblue fruit.

JAMES JOYCE

The moment one gives close attention to anything, even a blade of grass, it becomes a mysterious, awesome indescribably magnificent world in itself.

HENRY MILLER

This we know: the earth does not belong to man, man belongs to the earth. All things are connected like the blood that unites us all. Man did not weave the web of life, he is merely a strand in it. Whatever he does to the web, he does to himself.

CHIEF SEATTLE

I was and still am puzzled by the fact that the wind blows preferably from the west in our latitudes. Once I asked a famous meteorologist for an explanation. He asked me to come to his office, where he showed me his computer outputs calculating the wind directions, taking into account the solar radiation, the rotation of the earth, and other important facts. "You see," he said, "all the arrows in the middle latitudes point west to east." I replied, "Now the computer understands it, but what about you and me?"

VICTOR WEISSKOPF

Atoms are so small and there are so many of them. For example, in your last breath it is almost certain that you have inhaled one atom from the dying breath of Julius Caesar as he lamented "Et tu, Brute," That is scientific trivia. But the fact is that a human breath contains about one million billion billion atoms. Even if they mix with the entire atmosphere of the earth, the chances are high that you will inhale on of them.

HEINZ PAGELS

Nature, it seems, is the popular name for milliards and milliards and milliards of particles playing their infinite game of billiards and billiards and billiards.

PIET HEIN

I am, as it were an eye that the cosmos uses to look at itself. The Mind is not mine alone; the Mind is everywhere.

RUDY RUCKER

I have remembered more than I have seen.

BENJAMIN DISRAELI

The nature of reality is this: it is hidden, and it is hidden, and it is hidden.

RUMI

The world is indeed only a small tide pool; disturb one part and the rest is threatened.

GREGORY BATESON

When you stop thinking that things have a past or future, and that they come or go, then in the whole universe there won't be a single atom that is not your own treasure.

HUIHAI

The world of learning is so broad, and the human soul is so limited in power! We reach forth and strain every nerve, but we seize only a bit of the curtain that hides the infinite from us.

MARIA MITCHELL

Alpha Centauri is the nearest star system to our Sun – 4.3 lightyears away. An Apollo spacecraft would take 850,000 years to reach the stars of Alpha Centauri. It would take a VW Rabbit 52 million years to make the same trip at 55 miles per hour, which is equal to 722,000 average lifetimes.

NEIL MCALEER

Raum. If there were one word it would be Raum. The space of things. The space of outer space. The space of night which comes through porous windows to feed on our faces. The mystical carpet where lovers wrestle ... Not just the room in which the furniture of the world rests, but the space of the things themselves. The space made by Being's breathing ... Not just the space we call conscious-ness, but the space where we retire in order to avoid a feeling, the touch of a lover, the plea of a friend, the threat of intimacy. Dis-tance. Darkness dotted by stars.

WILLIAM GASS

It has taken biologists some 230 years to identify and describe three quarters of a million insects; if there are indeed at least thirty million, as Terry Erwin of the Smithsonian Institute estimates, then, working as they have in the past, insect taxonomists have ten thou-sand years of employment ahead of them.

RICHARD LEAKEY AND ROGER LEWIN

To me it is enough to wonder at the secrets.

ALBERT EINSTEIN

Don't be confused by surfaces; in the depths everything becomes law.

RAINER MARIA RILKE

Don't bring the ocean if I feel thirsty, nor heaven if I ask for a light; but bring a hint, some dew, a particle, as birds carry only drops away from water, and the wind a grain of salt.

OLAV H. HAUGE

But what is letting go? I think we don't understand it at all. We've got this idea of something trapped that we've got to set free. Like there's a bird in your hand, and what Zen is about is spreading your fingers and letting it fly away. Whoosh! I'm enlightened! But you and the bird are the same! You and your hand are the same! Nothing needs to be opened! Nothing needs to fly away! Realize this and you've automatically let go.

BERNARD GLASSMAN

The world faces us with the impossibility of knowing it directly ... It is a world whose nature cannot be comprehended by our human powers of mental conception.

MAX PLANCK

It seems to me that the mysterious thing about nature is not that it is comprehensible but that it contains such a thing as comprehension at all.

JONATHAN MILLER

We must endure our thoughts all night, until the bright obvious stands motionless in the cold.

WALLACE STEVENS

Of all that God has shown me I can speak just the smallest word, not more than a honeybee takes on her foot from an overspilling jar.

MECHTHILD OF MAGDEBURG

To my mind, the laws which nature obeys are less suggestive of those which a machine obeys in its motion than those which a musician obeys in writing a fugue, or a poet in composing a sonnet.

SIR JAMES JEANS

The choice is: the universe ... or nothing.

H.G WELLS

But there is another way of seeing that involves a letting go. When I see this way I sway transfixed and emptied. The difference between the two ways of seeing is the difference between walking with and without a camera. When I walk with a camera I walk from shot to shot, reading the light on a calibrated meter. When I walk without a camera, my own shutter opens, and the moment's light prints on my own silver gut. When I see this second way I am above all an unscrupulous observer.

ANNIE DILLARD

Life is not made of the number of breaths we take, but of the moments that take our breath away.

SOURCE UNKNOWN

Light, too, has unknowable qualities. We never see light itself. The light that strikes the eye is known only through the energy it releases. This energy is translated into a visual image in the mind. Although the image appears to be composed of light, the light we see is a quality appearing in consciousness. What light actually is, we never know directly.

PETER RUSSELL

The surest test if a man be sane is if he accepts life whole, as it is, without needing by measure or touch to understand the measureless untouchable source of its image.

LAOTZU

The star could not, by itself, become aware of its own beauty or sacrifice. But the star can, through us, reflect back on itself. In a sense, you are the star. Look at your hand – do you claim it as your own? Your eyes, your brain, your bones, all of you is composed of the star's creations. You are that star, brought into a form of life that enables life to reflect on itself.

BRIAN SWIMME

Dust as we are, the immortal spirit grows like harmony in music; there is a dark inscrutable workmanship that reconciles discordant elements, makes them cling together in one society.

WILLIAM WORDSWORTH

One world at a time.

HENRI DAVID THOREAU, ON BEING ASKED
HIS OPINION OF THE HEREAFTER.

The scientist does not defy the universe. He accepts it. It is his dish to savor, his realm to explore; it is his adventure and neverending delight. It is complaisant and elusive but never dull. It is wonderful both in the small and in the large. In short, its exploration is the highest occupation for a gentleman.

I.I. RABI

I believe that life can go on forever. It takes a million years to evolve a new species, ten million for a new genus, one hundred million for a class, a billion for a phylum, and that's usually as far as your imagination goes. In a billion years, it seems intelligent life might be as different from humans as humans are from insects. But what would happen in another ten billion years? It's utterly impossible to conceive of ourselves changing as drastically as that, over and over again. All you can say is, on that kind of time scale the material form that life would take is completely open. To change from a human being to a cloud may seem a big order but it's the kind of change you'd expect over billions of years.

FREEMAN DYSON

It is quite possible that mathematics was invented in the ancient Middle East to keep track of tax receipts and grain stores. How odd that out of this should come a subtle scientific language that can effectively describe and predict the most arcane aspects of the Universe.

ISAAC ASIMOV

How could our eyes see the sun, unless they were sunlike themselves?

JOHANN WOLFGANG VON GOETHE

It seems the yard wants to be a meadow. So if we wait – and we can since time today does not exist – we can go there, to lie in a sunny meadow until twilight, when nearby pines make a sheltering bed, home to the howling dog and the broken heart. And where starlight excites the treetops which shiver to be alive.

ROSLYN NELSON

If you try to know it, you have already departed from it.

CHUANG TZU

I often dream about falling ... lately I dreamed I was clutching at the face of a rock but it would not hold. Gravel gave way. I grasped for a shrub, but it pulled loose, and in cold terror I fell into the abyss. Suddenly ... a feeling of pleasure overcame me. I realized that what I embody, the principle of life, cannot be destroyed ... As I continued to fall in the dark void, embraced by the vault of the heavens, I sang to the beauty of the stars and made my peace with the darkness.

HEINZ R. PAGELS

It goes against nature in a large field to grow only one shaft of wheat and in an infinite universe to have only one living world.

METRODORUS OF CHIOS 400 B.C.

The universe shivers with wonder in the depths of the human. Do you see? Think of what it would be like if there were no humans on the planet: the mountains and the primeval fireball would be magnificent, but the Earth would not feel any of this.

BRIAN SWIMME

What's fire? You can tell me about oxidation, but that doesn't tell me a thing.

JOSEPH CAMPBELL

Give me the ninetytwo elements and I'll give you a universe. Ubiquitous hydrogen. Standoffish helium. Spooky boron. Nononsense carbon. Promiscuous oxygen. Faithful iron. Mysterious phosphorous. Exotic xenon. Brash tin. Slippery mercury. Heavyfooted lead. Imagine, if you will, a chemical storeroom stocked with the ninetytwo elements. Pop the corks, open the valves, tip over the boxes and canisters. Watch what happens.

CHET RAYMO

What really interests me is whether God had any choice in the creation of the world.

ALBERT EINSTEIN

I don't think there is one unique universe ... Even the laws of physics themselves may be somewhat observer dependent.

STEPHEN HAWKING

Put three grains of sand inside a vast cathedral, and the cathedral will be more closely packed with sand than space is with stars.

SIR JAMES JEANS

The world is so exquisite, with so much love and moral depth, that there is no reason to deceive ourselves with pretty stories for which there's little good evidence. Far better, it seems to me, in our vulnerability, is to look Death in the eye and to be grateful every day for the brief but magnificent opportunity that life provides.

CARL SAGAN

How is it that the sky feeds the stars?

LUCRETIUS

One day, during the midst of my questions, I took my twoyearold daughter to the ocean for the first time. It was a mild, slightly hazy day in June. We parked our car a half mile from the water and walked toward the coast. A speckled pink crab shell lay on the sand and caught her attention. A hundred yards farther, we heard the rolling of the waves, in rhythmical sequence, and I could tell that my daughter was curious about what made the sound. Holding her up with one arm, I pointed to the sea. My daughter's eyes followed along my arm across the beach, and then out to the vast bluegreen ocean. For a moment she hesitated. I wasn't sure whether she would be puzzled or frightened by that first sight of infinity. Then she broke out into a radiant smile. There was nothing I needed to say to her, nothing I needed to explain.

ALAN LIGHTMAN

"What should we do about that moon?" Seems to Hafiz most everyone has laid aside the music tackling such profoundly useless questions.

HAFIZ

By the act of observation we may have selected a "real" history out of the many realities, and once someone has seen a tree in our world it stays there even when nobody is looking at it.

JOHN GRIBBIN

A well known scientist (some say it was Bertrand Russell) once gave a public lecture on astronomy. He described how the earth orbits around the sun and how the sun in turn orbits around the center of a vast collection of stars called our galaxy. At the end of the lecture, a little old lady at the back of the room got up and said: "What you have told us is rubbish. The world is really a flat plane supported on the back of a giant tortoise." The scientist gave a superior smile before replying, "What is the tortoise standing on?" "You're very clever, young man, very clever," said the old lady. "But it's turtles all the way down."

STEPHEN HAWKING

We are like lutes once held by God. Being away from his warm body fully explains this constant yearning.

HAFIZ

We have two eyes to see two sides of things, but there must be a third eye which will see everything at the same time and yet not see anything.

D.T. SUZUKI

What a remarkable idea, that when you accelerate into a run, your muscles are fighting the influence of galaxies scarcely visible even with the most powerful telescopes!

B.K. RIDLEY

Be – and yet know the great void where all things begin, the infinite source of your own most intense vibration, so that, this once, you may give it your perfect assent.

RAINER MARIA RILKE

Though the bamboo forest is dense, water flows through it freely.

ZEN SAYING

Antiprotons are so small that one quadrillion – that's 1,000,000,000,000,000 – would occupy a space 30,000 times smaller than the period at the end of this sentence.

SOURCE UNKNOWN

In Highland New Guinea, now Papua New Guinea, a British district officer named James Taylor contacted a mountain village, above three thousand feet, whose tribe had never seen any trace of the outside world. It was the 1930's. He described the courage of one villager. One day, on the airstrip hacked from the mountains near his village, this man cut vines and lashed himself to the fuselage of Taylor's airplane shortly before it took off. He explained calmly to his loved ones that, no matter what happened to him, he had to see where it came from.

    ANNIE DILLARD

He cannot turn back who is tied to a star.

    LEONARDO DA VINCI

There is no means of proving it is preferable to be than not to be.

    E.M. CIORAN

By watching, I know that the stars are not going to last. I have seen some of the best ones melt and run down the sky. Since one can melt, they can all melt; since they can all melt, they can all melt the same night. That sorrow will come – I know it. I mean to sit up every night and look at them as long as I can keep awake; and I will impress those sparkling fields on my memory, so that by and by when they are taken away I can by my fancy restore those lovely myriads to the black sky and make them sparkle again, and double them by the blur of my tears.

    MARK TWAIN

With all your science, can you tell how it is, and whence it is, that light comes into the soul?

    HENRY DAVID THOREAU

There are many things about which you can ask, "What is its temperature?" or "What color is it?" but you may not ask the temperature question or the color question of, say, jealousy or prayer. Similarly, you are right to ask the "Why" question of a bicycle's mudguards or the Kariba Dam, but at the very least you have no right to assume that the "Why" question deserves an answer when posed about a boulder, a misfortune, Mt. Everest or the universe.

    RICHARD DAWKINS

All things die and all things live forever; but our task is to die, to die making roads, roads over the sea. To die...To fall like a drop of sea water into the immense sea? Or to be what I have never been: one man, without shadow, without dream, a man all alone, walking with no road, with no mirror?

ANTONIO MACHADO

God is trying to sell you something, but you don't want to buy. That is what your suffering is: Your fantastic haggling, your manic screaming over the price!

HAFIZ

The unrest which keeps the neverstopping clock of metaphysics going is the thought that the nonexistence of this world is just as possible as its existence.

WILLIAM JAMES

Science cannot solve the ultimate mystery of Nature. And it is because in the last analysis we ourselves are part of the mystery we are trying to solve.

MAX PLANCK

The black holes of nature are the most perfect macroscopic objects there are in the universe: the only elements in their construction are our concepts of space and time.

S. CHANDRASHEKAR

My favorite piece of music is the one we hear all the time if we are quiet.

JOHN CAGE

The Hindu teacher Swami Muktananda was once asked why he didn't work miracles. He replied, "I have no need to work miracles. The circulation of blood through my body is enough."

Neutrinos are streaming through your body as you read this. Over a trillion neutrinos from the Sun stream through your body at near the speed of light every single second of every single day.

LAWRENCE M. KRAUSS

Some day comes the Great Awakening when we realize that this life is no more than a dream. Yet the foolish go on thinking they are awake: Surveying the panorama of life with such clarity, they call this one a prince and that one a peasant – What delusion! The great Confucius and you are both a dream. And I, who say all this is a dream. I, too, am a dream.

CHUANG TZU

The river is moving. The blackbird must be flying.

WALLACE STEVENS

All of this is the Earth educating itself. Think of the language that has come alive in just this one afternoon: do you think we are solely responsible for that? Good heavens, no! Think of the sacrifices required of billions of creatures to make such language possible. Take a single sentence: "The fireball exploded twenty billion years ago at the beginning of time." That sentence required nothing less than the full twenty billion years of cosmic development. It is not "my" sentence; nor does it "belong" to the theoretical scientists who first predicted the existence of the fireball, nor the experimental scientists who first detected its heat; it is a sentence of the whole Earth. Nothing less than that is required for its speaking forth. The sentence could not exist without the oceans, the rivers, the air, the life forms, and all the thousands of years of human cultural activities. Every sentence is spoken by the whole Earth.

BRIAN SWIMME

How do I know that loving life is not a delusion? How do I know that in hating death I am not like a man who, having left home in his youth, has forgotten the way back?

CHUANGTZU

When did smoke learn how to fly?

PABLO NERUDA

The world is ruled by letting things take their course.

LAOTZU

And so, multileveled Mother Nature, wry and cruel but at times strangely benevolent, has inserted a mechanism in the mechanism to prevent that mechanism from fully comprehending its mechanistic nature. Faith itself, in other words, is but a mechanism.

JON FRANKLIN

By convention sweet is sweet, by convention bitter is bitter, by convention hot is hot, by convention cold is cold, by convention color is color. But in reality there are only atoms and the void.

DEMOCRITUS 500 B.C.

If you want the truth, I'll tell you the truth: Listen to the secret sound, the real sound, which is inside you. The one no one talks of speaks the secret sound to himself, and he is the one who has made it all.

KABIR

As we acquire more knowledge, things do not become more comprehensible, but more mysterious.

WILL DURANT

Not known, because not looked for but heard, half heard, in the stillness between two waves of the sea. Quick now, here, not, always – a condition of complete simplicity (Costing not less than everything).

T.S. ELIOT

It is in the unearthly first hour of twilight that earth's almost agonized livingness is felt. This hour is so dreadful to some people that they hurry indoors to turn on the lights.

ELIZABETH BOWEN

A windup toy unwinds and lightens by one billionth the weight of the dot of an i ... The sun shines for 1 second and loses the weight of 2 dozen ocean liners.

PHILIP AND PHYLIS MORRISON

The really hard problem is consciousness itself. Why should the complex processing of information in the brain lead to an inner experience? Why doesn't it all go on in the dark, without any subjective aspect? Why do we have any inner life at all?

PETER RUSSELL

I cannot say which is which: the glowing plum blossom is the spring night's moon.

IZUMI SHIKIBU

In some sense man is a microcosm of the universe, therefore what man is, is a clue to the universe. We are enfolded in the universe.

DAVID BOHM

Pulling out the chair beneath your mind and watching you fall upon God – what else is there for Hafiz to do that is any fun in this world!

HAFIZ

During World War II, St. Petersburg was surrounded by the Germany army and cut off from other parts of Russia for months. Finally, there was no food. No heat. Just the sound of the German bombings. But the people of St. Petersburg did not surrender. They were determined not to give up their city. The radio DJ tried to cheer people up by playing music, talking and cracking jokes. Finally, he became lethargic as well. Nevertheless, he felt he could still do something to help people survive. He let a metronome tick live on the radio. People lay down and just listened and held on to that sound of the metronome ticking through day and night. That's how St. Petersburg managed not to fall.

YOKO ONO

In a wellknown instance involving Dutch botanists who were exploring the plants of the coastal plain with local Arawak Indians as guides, the botanists were either overzealous in their note taking or completely baffled by the local language. Published accounts detailing that area's flora list a long Arawak name for one of the species. When translated into English, it means "I don't know this one so I'll have to ask my uncle."

MARK PLOTKIN

You realize beyond all trace of doubt that the world is in you, and not you in the world.

SRI NISARGADATTA MAHARAJ

I circle around God, around the primordial tower. I've been circling for thousands of years and I still don't know: am I a falcon, a storm, or a great song?

RAINER MARIA RILKE

One of the most remarkable astrophysical facts I know of is that essentially every atom inside our bodies was once inside an exploding star. The carbon that permeates our bodies, the oxygen and nitrogen we breathe, were not around when matter first formed. These elements were created in the nuclear furnaces of stars. In order for us to exist, it was necessary for generations of massive stars to live and die. Perhaps, in one way or another, we may someday return the favor.

LAWRENCE M. KRAUS

The Lurianic Cabalists were vexed by the question of how God could have created anything, since He was already everywhere and hence there could have been no room anywhere for His creation. In order to approach this mystery, they conceived the notion of tsimtsum, which means a sort of holding in of breath. Luria suggested that at the moment of creation God, in effect, breathed in – He absented Himself; or, rather, He hid Himself; or, rather, He entered into Himself – so as to make room for His creation.

LAWRENCE WESCHLER

A grassblade's no easier to make than an oak.

JAMES RUSSELL LOWELL

All that each person is, and experiences, and shall never experience, in body and in mind, all these things are differing expressions of himself and of one root, and are identical: and not one of these things nor one of these persons is ever quite to be duplicated, nor replaced, nor has it ever quite had precedent; but each is a new and incommunicably tender life, wounded in every breath, and almost as hardly killed as easily wounded: sustaining for a while, without defense, the enormous assaults of the universe.

JAMES AGEE

One ought to be ashamed to make use of the wonders of science embodied in a radio set, while appreciating them as little as a cow appreciates the botanical marvels in the plant she munches.

ALBERT EINSTEIN

The story goes that the incomparable Buckminster Fuller was asked one day, near the end of his life, whether he was finally disappointed, having done so much to bring about the era of space travel, that he himself would never be able to experience outer space. To which the old man magisterially replied, "But, Sir, we are in outer space."

LAWRENCE WESCHLER

Nothing in the world, no object or event, would be true or false if there were not thinking creatures.

DONALD DAVIDSON

Perhaps the immense Milky Way which on clear nights we behold stretching across the heavens, this vast encircling ring in which our planetary system is itself but a molecule, is in turn but a cell in the Universe, in the Body of God.

MIGUEL DE UNAMUNO

An obscure moth from Latin America saved Australia's pastureland from overgrowth by cactus ... the rosy periwinkle provided the cure for Hodgkin's disease and childhood lymphocytic leukemia .. the bark of the Pacific yew offers hope for victims of ovarian and breast cancer ... a chemical from the saliva of leeches dissolves blood clots during surgery.

EDWARD G. WILSON

The moon bird's head is filled with nothing but thoughts of the moon and when the next rain will come is all that the rain bird thinks of. Who is it we spend our entire life loving?

KABIR

There is a crack in everything God has made.

RALPH WALDO EMERSON

The rain screws up its face and falls to bits. Then it makes itself again. Only the rain can make itself again.

ADRIAN KEITH SMITH, AGE 4

If we follow a particular recipe, word for word, in a cookery book, what finally emerges from the oven is a cake. We cannot break the cake into its component crumbs and say: this crumb corresponds to the first word in the recipe; this crumb corresponds to the second word in the recipe.

RICHARD DAWKINS

I laid my heart open to the benign indifference of the universe.

ALBERT CAMUS

I am entirely on the side of the mystery. I mean, any attempts to explain away the mystery is ridiculous … I believe in the profound and unfathomable mystery of life.

ALDOUS HUXLEY

Quarks are located in a physical "somewhere" between matter and spirit … The "inconceivable concept" of the electron as a "wave of matter" alone touches upon a metaphysical dimension … These "waves of matter" are more than shape; they are metashape, shapes to which we can no longer attribute a substantial content – only a spiritual one.

GERHARD STAGUHN

Watching the moon at dawn, solitary, midsky, I knew myself completely: no part left out.

IZUMI SHIKIBU

Try and penetrate with out limited means the secrets of nature and you will find that, behind all the discernible concatenations, there remains something subtle, intangible and inexplicable. Veneration for this force beyond anything that we can comprehend is my religion.

ALBERT EINSTEIN

You have said what you are. I am what I am. Your actions in my head, my head here in my hands with something circling inside. I have no name for what circles so perfectly.

RUMI

Deep in my looking, the last words vanished. Joyous and silent, the waking that met me there.

LAL DED

We look at the world rather as an overworked executive looks at a stranger who is probably about to ask him a favor. Yet we only become aware of this in those moments of acceptance when we find ourselves looking at everything with sympathetic interest. This, I realized, was what the German poet Rilke had meant by the phrase "dennoch preisen" – to praise in spite of. Rilke been impressed by Baudelaire's poem "Carrion," describing how the poet and his mistress come upon the horrible rotting carcass of a dog in a public park, because it made poetry out of something normally considered too disgusting to mention. Rilke saw, in a flash of insight, that this is the real business of the poet: to raise himself to a level of mental intensity where everything in the world, even a rotting carcass, becomes fascinating.

COLIN WILSON

A Taoist master was sitting naked in his mountain cabin, meditating. A group of Confucianists entered the door of his hut, having hiked up the mountain intending to lecture him on the rules of proper conduct. When they saw the sage sitting naked before them, they were shocked, and asked, "What are you doing, sitting in your hut without any pants on?" The sage replied, "This entire universe is my hut. This little hut is my pants. What are you fellows doing inside my pants?"

JAMES N. POWELL

At the outset of rational doubt twentyfive hundred years ago, Plato suggested that there was little difference between imagination and reality. He observed that anything that one could reasonably imagine was eventually possible. The plenum of the mind, according to Plato, is actually the cornucopia of reality. In agreement, William Blake penned, "Everything possible to be believ'd is an image of truth."

SOURCE UNKNOWN

Nature loves to hide.

HERACLITUS

I know what the greatest cure is: it is to give up, to relinquish, to surrender, so that our little hearts may beat in unison with the great heart of the world.

HENRY MILLER

We cannot doubt the existence of an ultimate reality. It is the universe forever masked. We are part of it, and the masks figured by us are the universe observing and understanding itself from a human point of view.

WARD HARRISON

The universe seen from within is light; seen from without, by spiritual perception, it is thought.

RUDOLF STEINER

The universe seems to me infinitely strange and foreign. At such a moment I gaze upon it with a mixture of anguish and euphoria; separate from the universe, as though placed at a certain distance outside it; I look and I see pictures, creatures that move in a kind of timeless time and spaceless space, emitting sounds that are a kind of language I no longer understand or even register.

EUGENE IONESCO

You are sitting on the earth and you realize that this earth deserves you and you deserve the earth. You are there – fully, personally, genuinely.

CHOGYAM TRUNGPA

I must now openly state my own bias and say that I do not believe in Chance; I believe in Providence and Miracles. If photosynthesis was invented by chance, then I can only say it was a damned lucky chance for us. If, biologically speaking, it is a statistical impossibility that I should be walking the earth instead of a million other possible people, I can only think of it as a miracle which I must do my best to deserve.

LOREN EISELEY

Spend the afternoon. You can't take it with you.

ANNIE DILLARD

Maybe he was asleep in the bath. The particle world is the dream world of the intelligence officer. An electron can be here or there at the same moment. You can choose; it can go from here to there without going in between; it can pass through two doors at the same time, or from one door to another by a path which is there for all to see until someone looks, and then the act of looking has made it take a different path. Its movement cannot be anticipated because it has no reasons. It defeats surveillance because when you know what it's doing you can't be certain where it is, and when you know where it is you can't be certain what it's doing: Heisenberg's uncertainty principle; and this is not because you're not looking carefully enough, it is because there is no such thing as an electron with a definite position and a definite momentum; you fix one, you lose the other, and it's all done without tricks, it's the real world, it is awake.

TOM STOPPARD

The group included some of the best nuclear physicists in the country. They knew something about highfrequency radiation from their work on cyclotrons, but the magnetron confounded even them at first. "It's simple," Isidore Rabi told the theorists who were seated around a table staring at the disassembled parts of the tube. "It's just a kind of whistle." "Okay, Rabi," Edward U. Condon asked, "how does a whistle work?" Rabi was at a loss for a satisfactory explanation.

DANIEL J. KEVLES

Sow in me your living breath, as you sow a seed in the earth.

KADYA MOLODOWSKY

The totality of our socalled knowledge or beliefs, from the most casual matters of geography and history to the profoundest laws of atomic physics or even of pure mathematics and logic, is a man-made fabric.

W.V.O. QUINE

You look out at the sky, and you look at Jupiter. It brings in all of us the same wonder, the same awe about the universe. I think the astronomer has more awe and wonder because he knows what it is that is up there. His knowledge doesn't diminish his awe; it enhances it.

MAXINE SINGER

The Universe is full of magical things, patiently waiting for our wits to grow sharper.

EDEN PHILLPOTTS

I'll tell you how the sun rose a ribbon at a time.

EMILY DICKINSON

I have to admit that sometimes nature seems more beautiful than strictly necessary. Outside the window of my home office there is a hackberry tree, visited frequently by a convocation of politic birds: blue jays, yellowthroated vireos, and, loveliest of all, an occasional red cardinal. Although I understand pretty well how brightly colored feathers evolved out of a competition for mates, it is almost irresistible to imagine that all this beauty was somehow laid out for our benefit.

STEVEN WEINBERG

God speaks to each of us as he make us, then walks with us silently out of the night. These are the words we dimly hear: You, sent out beyond your recall, go to the limits of your longing. Embody me.

RAINER MARIA RILKE

To me every hour of the light and dark is a miracle, every cubic inch of space is a miracle.

WALT WHITMAN

The sun rises. In that short phrase, in a single fact, is enough information to keep biology, physics, and philosophy busy for the rest of time.

LYALL WATSON

A human being is part of the whole, called by us "Universe"; a part limited in time and space. He experiences himself, his thoughts and feelings as some thing separated from the rest – a kind of optical delusion of his consciousness. This delusion is a kind of prison for us, restricting us to our personal desires and to affection for a few persons nearest us. Our task must be to free ourselves from this prison by widening our circle of compassion to embrace all living creatures and the whole of nature in its beauty.

TIMOTHY FERRIS

...the rules of clockwork might apply to familiar objects such as snookerballs, but when it comes to atoms, the rules are those of roulette.

PAUL DAVIES

Nature uses only the longest threads to weave her patterns, so each small piece of her fabric reveals the organization of the entire tapestry.

RICHARD FEYNMAN

We are traveling with tremendous speed toward a star in the Milky Way. A great repose is visible on the face of the earth. My heart's a little fast. Otherwise everything is fine.

BERTOLT BRECHT

I have no doubt that in reality the future will be vastly more surprising than anything I can imagine. Now my own suspicion is that the universe is not only queerer than we suppose, but queerer than we can suppose.

J.B.S. HALDANE

So that how it can be that a stone, a plant, a star, can take on the burden of being; and how it is that a child can take on the burden of breathing; and how through so long a continuation and cumulation of the burden of each moment one on another, does any creature bear to exist, and not break utterly to fragments of nothing: these are matters too dreadful and fortitudes too gigantic to meditate long and not forever to worship.

JAMES AGEE

Whatever light is, it seems to exist in a realm where there is no before and no after. There is only now.

PETER RUSSELL

"Only we must begin quick. It's getting as dark as it can." "And darker," said Tweedledee.

LEWIS CARROLL

Things are not what they seem to be, nor are they otherwise.

LANKAVATARA SUTRA

When we try to pick out anything by itself, we find it hitched to everything else in the universe.

JOHN MUIR

The dismay that may be aroused by our inability to answer questions about first and last things is something which ordinary people have long since worked out for themselves. Voltaire's remedy: "We must cultivate our garden."

PETER MEDAWAR

Ever splitting the light! How often do they strive to divide that which, despite everything, would always remain single and whole.

GOETHE

Now we will count to twelve and we will all keep still for once on the face of the earth, let's not speak in any language; let's stop for a second, and not move our arms so much.

PABLO NERUDA

Cycles of light and dark, of heat and cold, of magnetism, radio-activity, and gravity all provide vital guides – and life learns to respond to even their most subtle signs. The emergence of a fruitfly is tuned by a spark lasting one thousandth of a second; the breeding of a bristle worm is coordinated on the ocean floor by a glimmer of light reflected from the moon ... Nothing happens in isolation. We breathe and bleed, we laugh and cry, we crash and die in time with cosmic cues.

LYALL WATSON

Kilgore Trout once wrote a short story which was a dialogue between two pieces of yeast. They were discussing the possible purposes of life as they ate sugar and suffocated in their own excrement. Because of their limited intelligence, they never came close to guessing that they were making champagne.

KURT VONNEGUT

God is a pure nothing, concealed in now and here: the less you reach for him, the more he will appear.

ANGELUS SILESIUS

We are the night ocean filled with glints of light. We are the space between the fish and the moon, while we sit here together.

RUMI

If any elderly but distinguished scientist says that something is possible he is almost certainly right, but if he says that it is impossible he is very probably wrong.

ARTHUR C. CLARKE

I believe in the incomprehensibility of God.

HONORE BALZAC

The common division of the world into subject and object, inner world and outer world, body and soul, is no longer adequate and leads us into difficulties.

WERNER HEISENBERG

The concept of an instrument that can look to the far reaches of the universe and say something about what it means to be human – that touches everyone. It's an incredibly romantic idea.

STORY MUSGRAVE

our "now" is not my "now.

CHARLES LAMB

The universe contains vastly more order than earthlife could every demand. All those distant galaxies, irrelevant for our existence, seem as equally well ordered as our own.

PAUL DAVIES

If our solar system (the Sun and nine planets) could fit into a coffee cup, our Galaxy would be the size of North America. Our Galaxy has a diameter of at least 80,000 lightyears – that is, 480 million billion miles.

NEIL MCALEER

Every Grain of sand, every tip of a leaf, even an atom contains the entire universe. Conversely, the universe can be perceived as the tip of a leaf.

GERHARD STAGUHN

Einstein's space is no closer to reality than Van Gogh's sky.

ARTHUR KOESTLER

I believe that scientific knowledge has fractal properties; that no matter how much we learn, whatever is left, however small it may seem, is just as infinitely complex as the whole was to start with. That, I think, is the secret of the Universe.

ISAAC ASIMOV

There the eye goes not, speech goes not, nor the mind.
The Upanishads
What else is going on right his minute while ground water creeps under my feet? The galaxy is careening in a slow, muffled widening. If a million solar systems are born every hour, then surely hundreds burst into being as I shift my weight to the other elbow.

ANNIE DILLARD

In the new theories of physicists, the fundamental material particles – protons, neutrons, electrons – dissolve into a kind of cosmic music, all resonances, vibrations, and spooky entanglements. Matter has revealed itself as a thing of astonishing, almost immaterial subtlety. The one property of matter that lingers is its potentiality. The hydrogen and helium atoms forged in the Big Bang possessed a builtin capacity to complexify and diversify, to spin out stars and galaxies, carbon silicon, oxygen, iron, and ultimately the tricky substrate of the Earth, even life and consciousness. Far from explaining away the mystery of the world, our new knowledge of matter rubs our noses in mystery.

CHET RAYMO

The difference between the lifeblood of plants and people is but one atom: Chlorophyll is made of 136 atoms of hydrogen, carbon, oxygen, and nitrogen arranged in a ring around a single atom of magnesium: hemoglobin (blood) is made up of 136 atoms of hydrogen, carbon, oxygen and nitrogen arranged in a ring around a single atom of iron.

ANNIE DILLARD

Laurens van der Post reports that Bushmen speak of someone's death like this: "The sound which used to ring in the sky for him no longer rings."

I confess I do not believe in time. I like to fold my magic carpet, after use, in such a way as to superimpose one part of the pattern upon another. Let visitors trip. And the highest enjoyment of timelessness – in a landscape selected at random – is when I stand among rare butterflies and their food plants. This is ecstasy, and behind the ecstasy is something else, which is hard to explain.

VLADIMIR NABOKOV

To live is so startling it leaves little time for anything else.

EMILY DICKINSON

Of course there is nothing the matter with the stars. It is my emptiness among them while they drift farther away in the invisible morning.

W.S. MERWIN

All that we do is touched with ocean, yet we remain on the shore of what we know.

RICHARD WILBUR

In the desire of the One to know its own beauty, we exist.

GHALIB

I see nothing but infinities on all sides which surround me as an atom, and as a shadow which endures only for an instant and it is no more.

BLAISE PASCAL

Earth, isn't this what you want: to arise within us, invisible? Isn't it your dream to be wholly invisible someday? – O Earth: invisible! What, if not transformation, is your urgent command? Earth, my dearest, I will. Oh believe me, you no longer need your springtimes to win me over – one of them, ah, even one, is already too much for my blood. Unspeakably I have belonged to you, from the first.

RAINER MARIA RILKE

Biology needs a better word than "error" for the driving force in evolution. Or maybe "error" will do after all, when you remember that it came from an old root meaning to wander about, looking for something.

LEWIS THOMAS

"So I wasn't dreaming, after all," she said to herself, "unless – unless we're all part of the same dream, and not the Red King's! I don't like belonging to another person's dream … I've a great mind to go and wake him, and see what happens."

LEWIS CARROLL

Would there be this eternal seeking if the found existed?
Antonio Porchia
The greatest mystery is not that we have been flung at random between the profusion of matter and of the stars, but that within this prison we can draw from ourselves images powerful enough to deny our nothingness.

ANDRE MALRAUX

I thought of a labyrinth of labyrinths, of one sinuous spreading labyrinth that would encompass the past and the future and in some way involve the stars.

JORGE LUIS BORGES

You and I are flesh and blood, but we are also stardust.

HELENA CURTIS

Everything is connected. Every electron to every other electron, every star to every other star. Muslims and Jews, bacteria and dinosaurs, plants and people – we all trace our language back to a common ancestor.

K.C. COLE

One day Chuga Chuangtzu and a friend were walking along a riverbank. "How delightfully the fishes are enjoying themselves in the water." Chuangtzu exclaimed. "You are not a fish," his friend said. "How do you know whether or not the fishes are enjoying themselves?" "You are not me," Chuangtzu said, "How do you know that I do not know that the fishes are enjoying themselves?

TAOIST MONDO

A scientific colleague tells me about a recent trip to the New Guinea highlands where she visited a Stone Age culture hardly contacted by Western civilization. They were ignorant of wristwatches, soft drinks, and frozen food. But they knew about Apollo 11. They knew that humans had walked on the Moon. They knew the names of Armstrong and Aldrin and Collins. They wanted to know who was visiting the Moon these days.

CARL SAGAN

Why is there something as opposed to nothing?

BERTRAND RUSSELL

I lived for thousands and thousands of years as a mineral and then I died and became a plant. And I lived for thousands and thousands of years as a plant and then I died and became an animal. And I lived for thousands and thousands of years as an animal and then I died and became a human being. Tell me, what have I ever lost by dying?

RUMI

Penetrating so many secrets, we cease to believe in the unknowable. But there it sits nevertheless, calmly licking its chops.

H.L. MENCKEN

One geneticist estimated that the difference between a mild virus and a killer can be as small as three atoms out of more than 5 million.

SOURCE UNKNOWN

We have little more personal stake in cosmic destiny than do sunflowers or butterflies. The transfiguration of the universe lies some 50 to 100 billion years in the future; snap your fingers twice and you will have consumed a greater fraction of your life than all human history is to such a span ... We owe our lives to universal processes ... and as invited guests we might do better to learn about them than to complain about them. If the prospect of a dying universe causes us anguish, it does so only because we can forecast it, and we have as yet not the slightest idea why such forecasts are possible for us ... Why should nature, whether hostile or benign, be in any way intelligible to us? All the mysteries of science are but palace guards to that mystery.

TIMOTHY FERRIS

What we observe is not nature itself, but nature exposed to our method of questioning.

WERNER HEISENBERG

If we want to solve a problem that we have never solved before, we must leave the door to the unknown ajar.

RICHARD FEYNMAN

The very fact that the universe is creative, and that the laws have permitted complex structures to emerge and develop to the point of consciousness – in other words, that the universe has organized its own selfawareness – is for me powerful evidence that there is "something going on" behind it all.

PAUL DAVIES

One of the most profound paradoxes of being human is that the thick spread of sensation we relish isn't perceived by the brain. The brain is silent, the brain is dark, the brain tastes nothing, the brain hears nothing. All it receives are electrical impulses – not the sumptuous chocolate melting sweetly, not the oboe solo like the flight of a bird, not the tingling caress, not the pastels of peach and lavender at sunset over a coral reef – just impulses. The brain is blind, deaf, dumb, unfeeling. The body is a transducer, a device that converts energy of one sort to energy of another sort, and that is its genius. Our bodies take mechanical energy and convert it to electrical energy. I touch the soft petal of a red rose called "Mr. Lincoln," and my receptors translate that mechanical touch into electrical impulses that the brain reads as soft, supple, thin, curled, dewy, velvety: rose petallike. When Walt Whitman said: I sing the body electric," he didn't know how prescient he was.

DIANE ACKERMAN

To get a universe that has expanded as long as ours has without either collapsing or having its matter coast away would have required extraordinary finetuning.

MICHAEL TURNER

Upon God himself, no man can think. And therefore I wish to leave everything I can think, and choose for my love that thing which I cannot think.

THE CLOUD OF UNKNOWING

Paul Eluard has a line about there being another world, but it's in this one. And Raymond Queneau said the world is not what it seems – but it isn't anything else either.

All of the material universe is comprised of subatomic particles. Not one of these particles, according to modern physics, can be "actualized," or made properly real, without an observation that collapses the wave function. Almost unbelievably, our most fundamental branch of science implies that what had previously been assumed to be a concrete, objective world cannot even be said to exist outside the subjective act of observation.

DAVID DARLING

For one who sets himself to look at all earnestly, at all in purpose toward truth, into the living eyes of a human life: what is it he there beholds that so freezes and abashes his ambitious heart? What is it, profound behind the outward windows of each one of you, beneath touch even of your own suspecting, drawn tightly back at bay against the backward wall and blackness of its prison cave, so that the eyes alone shine of their own angry glory, but the eyes of a trapped wild animal, or of a furious angel nailed to the ground by his wings, or however else one may faintly designate the human "soul?"

JAMES AGEE

The universe is like a safe to which there is a combination. But the combination is locked up in the safe.

PETER DE VRIES

The enormous night straining her waist against the Milky Way.

FEDERICO GARCIA LORCA

There is no such thing as an empty space or an empty time. There is always something to see, something to hear. In fact, try as we may to make a silence, we cannot. For certain engineering purposes, it is desirable to have as silent a situation as possible. Such a room is called an anechoic chamber, its six walls made of special material, a room without echoes. I entered one at Harvard University several years ago and heard two sounds, one high and one low. When I described them to the engineer in charge, he informed me that the high one was my nervous system in operation, the low one my blood in circulation.

JOHN CAGE

The only things that can be known are those compatible with the existence of knowers.

GEORGE GREENSTEIN

Our whole business in this life is to restore to health the eye of the heart whereby God may be seen.

AUGUSTINE

As you walk across the room, the number of invisible items imping-
ing upon your body is staggering. Besides the complete spectrum of
electromagnetic waves – the radio waves from nearby broadcast-
ing stations or from distant galaxies, the infrared waves radiated
by the heat of the walls or the bodies of other people in the room
– we are bombarded by invisible neutrinos from the Big Bang, gravi-
tational waves from collapsing stars in our galaxy, neutrons emitted by radioactive materials decaying in the ceiling and walls, not
to mention the invisible Higgs field that many elementary particle
physicists believe permeates space giving mass to all matter, or a
possible invisible field associated with the mysterious "dark matter" that is thought to make up the greater part of the mass of the
universe.

LAWRENCE M. KRAUSS

Let your thoughts flow past you, calmly; keep me near, at every
moment; trust me with your life, because I am you, more than you
yourself are.

THE BHAGAVAD GITA

I know perfectly well that at this moment the whole universe is listening to us, and that every word we say echoes to the remotest star.

JEAN GIRAUDOUX

If seeds in the black Earth can turn into such beautiful roses, what
might not the heart of man become in its long journey to the stars?

G.K. CHESTERTON

We turn to God for help when our foundations are shaking, only to
learn that it is God who is shaking them.

CHARLES C. WEST

"And so did Lao Tzu," I pushed on. "Yes, indeed: and so do the trees
over there. Logic won't do for them." "So what do they use instead?"
"Metaphor." "Metaphor?" "Yes, metaphor. That is how this whole
fabric of mental interconnections holds together. Metaphor is right
at the bottom of being alive."

FRITJOF CAPRA AND GREGORY BATESON

The advantage of the incomprehensible is that it never loses its freshness.

PAUL VALERY

Your mind is in every cell of your body.

CANDACE PERT

Our eye would have to be a trace more seeing, our ear more receptive, the taste of a fruit would have to penetrate us more completely, we would have to endure more odor, and in touching and being touched be more aware and less forgetful – in order promptly to absorb out of our immediate experiences consolations that would be more convincing, more preponderant, more true than all the suffering that can ever shake us to our very depths.

WILLIAM GASS

Step aside from all thinking, and there is nowhere you can't go.

SENGTS'AN

Quantum theory shows that nature cannot be separated from the person observing it. Quark theory suggests the existence of entities that can never be observed. By proposing that everything in the universe comes from nothing, the inflationary theory makes the disappearance of nature official. We are such things as dreams are made of, but who is doing the dreaming? "Now, Kitty," said Alice, "Let's consider who it was that dreamed it all. This is a serious question, my dear, and you should not go on licking your paws like that."

O.B. HARDISON, JR.

When poetry doesn't do it, scientists sometimes turn to music. Last month an international team of astronomers reported that a black hole lurking far away in the Perseus cluster of galaxies is creating rumbling vibrations of a certain pitch – B flat. This, however, would be B flat 57 octaves below middle C, toward the deep end of a piano keyboard some 50 feet long. This is a tone so low that each wave measures 30,000 light years from crest to crest (almost a third the length of the Milky Way). A single undulation takes 10 million years to complete.

NEWSPAPER

I cannot tell if the day is ending, or the world, or if the secret of secrets is inside me again.

ANNA AKHMATOVA

Nothing is more manifest than the hidden; nothing is more obvious than the unseen.

TZUSSU

To speak of man as "mastering" such a cosmos is about the equivalent of installing a grasshopper as Secretary General of the United Nations. Worse, in fact, for no matter what system of propulsion man may invent in the future, the galaxies on the outer rim of visibility are fleeing faster than he can approach them. Moreover, the light that he is receiving from them left its source in the early history of the planet earth. There is no possible way of even establishing their present existence. As the British astronomer Sir Bernard Lovell has so appropriately remarked, "At the limit of presentday observations our information is a few billion years out of date."

LOREN EISELEY

...life is tolerable only by the degree of mystification we endow it with.

E.M. CIORAN

Hours are leaves of life and I am their gardener ... Each hour falls down slow.

SUSAN MORRISON, AGE 11

Everything used to measure time really measures space.

JEROME DESHUSSES

When the Guest is being searched for, it is the intensity of the longing for the Guest that does all the work. Look at me, and you will see a slave of that intensity.

KABIR

We have found a strange footprint on the shores of the unknown. We have devised profound theories, one after another, to account for its origin. At last, we have succeeded in reconstructing the creature that made the footprint. And lo! It is our own.

SIR ARTHUR STANLEY EDDINGTON

The energy you use to read this sentence is powered, ultimately, by sunlight – perhaps first soaked up by some grass that got digested by a cow before it turned into the milk that made the cheese that topped the pizza. But sunlight, just the same.

K.C. COLE.

When you read or hear anything about the birth of the universe, someone is making it up ... only God knows what happened at the Very Beginning (and so far She hasn't let on).

LEON LEDERMAN

We wake suddenly in the middle of the night, and perceive infinite time exploding beyond us; we stare through the dark room at a universe that has existed for trillions of years before we were conceived. So macabre, so astonishing, so unlikely!

RICHARD GROSSINGER

Mind is like no other property of physical systems. It is not just that we don't know the mechanisms that give rise to it. We have difficulty seeing how any mechanism can give rise to it.

ERICH HARTH

We sit together, the mountain and me, until only the mountain remains.

LI PO

There is something very strange indeed about light. Whatever light is, it seems to exist in a realm where there is no before and no after. There is only now.

PETER RUSSELL

The ripe sweetness of summer dripped in beads from every tree and straight into my opened heart a tiny drop ran down.

EDITH SODERGRAN

"To see" means to taste and thereby to "dance the orange," to touch and feel at one's finger end a little eternity, to smell ourselves cloud like steam from a warm cup, to hear voices, to listen so intensely you rise straight from the ground.

WILLIAM GASS

"How can we ever hope to understand atoms?" Heisenberg had lamented that day. I think we may yet be able to do so," Bohr replied. "But in the process we may have to learn what the word 'understanding' really means."

Biological evolution also appears chaotic. Go back in time, kill one extra trilobite 500 millionmillion years ago, and perhaps human beings would never evolve – evolution could simply spin off in a different direction.

J. RICHARD GOTT

The wild geese do not intend to cast their reflections, the water has no mind to receive their images.

ZEN HAIKU

Anyone who, upon looking down at his bare feet, doesn't laugh, has either no sense of symmetry or no sense of humor.

DESCARTES

I'm an excitizen of nowhere, and sometimes I get homesick.

LEE MARVIN

I have been trying to think of the earth as a kind of organism but it is no go. I cannot think of it this way. It is too big, too complex, with too many working parts lacking visible connections. The other night, driving through a hilly, wooded part of southern New England, I wondered about this. If not like an organism, what is it like, what is it most like? Then, satisfactorily for that moment, it came to me: it is most like a single cell.

LEWIS THOMAS

Relativity and quantum theory have shown that is has no meaning to divide the observing apparatus from what is observed.

DAVID BOHM

Everything either is or is not.

ARISTOTLE

It isn't that a particle takes the path of least action but that it smells all the paths in the neighborhood and chooses the one that has the least action.

RICHARD FEYNMAN

Given so much time, the "impossible" becomes possible, the possible probable, and the probable virtually certain. One has only to wait: time itself performs miracles.

GEORGE WALD

Little by little, you will turn into stars.

HAFIZ

I asked her what sort of death I would die. She answered with a very tender smile: "God will sip you up like a little drop of dew."

WILLIAM STAFFORD

There the bee of the heart stays deep inside the flower, and cares for no other thing.

KABIR

Imagine the nucleus of an atom magnified to the size of a grain of rice. The whole atom would then be the size of a football stadium, and the electrons would be other grains of rice flying round the stands. As the early twentiethcentury British physicist Sir Arthur Eddington put it, "Matter is mostly ghostly empty space." To be more precise, it is 99,9999999 percent empty space.

PETER RUSSELL

"What's she doing?" I whispered to Dabe ... "She's asking the stars to take the little heart of her child and to give him something of the heart of a star in return." "But why the stars?" ... "Because, Moren," he said in a matteroffact tone, "The stars there have heart in plenty and are great hunters. She is asking them to take from her little child his little heart and to give him the heart of a hunter."

LAURENS VAN DER POST

I do take one hundred per cent seriously that the world is a figment of the imagination.

JOHN WHEELER

What am I to make of this? Universes as numerous as the bubbles that fizz from champagne! And I am barely getting used to this one. A single starry night is enough to make my head spin. One white orchid takes my breath away. Who am I to say if God exists or if this universe of galaxies is only a bubble of cosmic foam?

CHET RAYMO

Between the conscious and the unconscious, the mind has put up a swing: all earth creatures, even the supernovas, sway between these two trees, and it never winds down. Angels, animals, humans, insects by the million, also the wheeling sun and moon; ages go by, and it goes on. Everything is swinging: heaven, earth, water, fire, and the secret one slowly growing a body. Kabir saw that for fifteen seconds, and it made him a servant for life.

KABIR

God not only plays dice. He also sometimes throws the dice where they cannot be seen.

STEPHEN W. HAWKING

One of the most surprising recent advances in cosmology is that 75% of the Universe seems to be made of nothing.

CHARLES LINEWEAVER.

You'll climb trees. You won't be able to sleep, or need to, for the joy of it. Mornings, when light spreads over the pastures like wings, and fans a secret color into everything, and beats the trees sense-less with beauty, so you can't tell whether the beauty is in the trees – dazzling in cells like yellow sparks or green flashing water – or on them – a transfiguring silver air charged with the wings' invisible motion; mornings you won't be able to walk for the power of it …

ANNIE DILLARD

Why does the universe go to all the bother of existing?

STEPHEN W. HAWKING

This sense of the unfathomable beautiful ocean of existence drew me into science. I am awed by the universe, puzzled by it and sometimes angry at a natural order that brings such pain and suffering. Yet an emotion or feeling I have toward the cosmos seems to be reciprocated by neither benevolence nor hostility but just by silence. The universe appears to be a perfectly neutral screen unto which I can project any passion or attitude, and it supports them all.

HEINZ R. PAGELS

Though my soul may set in darkness, it will rise in perfect light; I have loved the stars too fondly to be fearful of the night.

SARAH WILLIAMS

What we take for the history of nature is only the very incomplete history of an instant.

DENIS DIDEROT

Man can only do what nature permits him to do. Man does not invent anything. He makes discoveries or principles operative in nature and often finds ways of reapplying them in surprise directions. That is called invention. But he does not do anything artificial. Nature has to permit it, and if nature permits it, it is natural.

R. BUCKMINSTER FULLER

Miracles rest simply upon our perceptions being made finer, so that for a moment our eyes can see and our ears can hear what there is about us always.

WILLA CATHER

What we know of the world comes to us primarily through vision. Our eyes, however, are sensitive only to that segment of the spectrum located between red and violet; the remaining 95 percent of all existing light (cosmic, infrared, ultraviolet, gammas, and Xrays) we cannot see. This means that we only perceive 5 percent of the "real" world.

AMOS VOGEL

I believe that there is, despite the fact that we humans have done so much damage to the world, a reason for our existence on this planet. I think we are here because the universe, with all its wonder and balance and logic, needs to be marveled at, and we are the only species (to our knowledge) that has the ability to do so. We are the one species that does not simply accept what is around us, and how it works. We are here because without us here to study it, the amazing complexity of the world would be wasted. And finally, we are here because the universe needs an entity to ask why it is here.

SARAH WESCHLER AGE 12

Flowers changed the face of the planet. Without them, the world we know – even man himself would never have existed … The weight of a petal has changed the face of the world and made it ours.

LOREN EISELEY

Thomas: When you see a candle's flame, you see the light from the candle. In that sense, we see the fireball. We are able to interact physically with photons from the beginning of time.
Youth: So we're in direct contact with the origin of the universe?
Thomas: That's right.

BRIAN SWIMME

The visible world is no longer a reality and the unseen world is no longer a dream.

WILLIAM BUTLER YEATS

We are the products of editing, rather than authorship.

GEORGE WALD

Every second, the earth is struck by 41/2 pounds of sunlight.

SOURCE UNKNOWN

The fact that the universe is governed by simple natural laws is remarkable, profound and on the face of it absurd. How can the vast variety in nature, the multitude of things and processes all be subject to a few simple, universal laws?

HEINZ R. PAGELS

From the side, a whole range; from the end, a single peak; far, near, high, low, no two parts alike. Why can't I tell the true shape of Lushan? Because I myself am in the mountain.

SU TUNGP'O

God is always opening his hand.

SPANISH PROVERB

News of the woman's hello, in electrical form, races along the neurons of the auditory nerve and enters the man's brain, through the thalamus, to a specialized region of the cerebral cortex for further processing. Eventually, a large fraction of the trillion neurons in the man's brain become involved with computing the visual and auditory date just acquired. Sodium and potassium gates open and close. Electrical currents speed along neuron fibers. Molecules flow from one nerve ending to the next. All of this is known. What is not known is why, after about a minute, the man walks over to the woman and smiles.

ALAN LIGHTMAN

I don't know exactly what prayer is. I do know how to pay attention, how to fall down into the grass, how to kneel down in the grass, how to be idle and blessed, how to stroll through the fields, which is what I have been doing all day. Tell me, what else should I have done? Doesn't everything die at last, and too soon? Tell me, what is it you plan to do with your one wild and precious life?

MARY OLIVER

Come here! Hurry! There are little animals in this rain water ... Look! See what I have discovered!

ANTONIE VAN LEEUWENHOEK, DUTCH MICROBIOLOGIST

For most of human history we have searched for our place in the cosmos. Who are we? We find that we inhabit an insignificant planet of a humdrum star lost in a galaxy tucked away in some forgotten corner of a universe in which there are far more galaxies than people. We make our world significant by the courage of our questions, and by the depth of our answers.

CARL SAGAN

Silverman's observation of convicts and schizophrenic patients make it clear that the trouble was that they had stopped noticing things, and finally stopped seeing them. They were not paying attention. A Zen parable tells how a common man asked the Zen Master Ikkyu to write down for him some maxims of the highest wisdom. The Master wrote one word: "Attention." "Will you not add something more?" asked the man, whereupon Ikkyu wrote, "Attention. Attention." The disgruntled man said he couldn't see much wisdom in this, where upon the Master wrote, "Attention. Attention. Attention." "What does attention mean?" asked the man, whereupon Ikkyu replied, "Attention means attention."

COLIN WILSON

The infinite quietness frightens me.

BLAISE PASCAL

The fairest thing we can experience is the mysterious. It is the fundamental emotion which stands at the cradle of true science. He who knows it not, and can no longer wonder, no longer feel amazement, is as good as dead. We all had this priceless talent when we were young. But as time goes by, many of us lose it. The true scientist never loses the faculty of amazement. It is the essence of his being.

HANS SELYE

You may never get to touch the Master, but you can tickle his creatures.

THOMAS PYNCHON

There is a theory which states that if ever anyone discovers exactly what the Universe is for and why it is here, it will instantly disappear and be replaced by something even more bizarre and inexplicable. There is another which states that this has already happened.

DOUGLAS ADAMS

By means of all created things, without exception, the divine assails us, penetrates us, and molds us. We imagined it as distant and inaccessible, whereas in fact we live steeped in its burning layers.

PIERRE TEILHARD DE CHARDIN

If you can look into the seeds of time, and say which grain will grow and which will not, speak then to me.

WILLIAM SHAKESPEARE

What's beautiful in science is that same thing that's beautiful in Beethoven. There's a fog of events and suddenly you see a connection. It … connects things that were always in you that were never put together before.

VICTOR WEISSKOPS

Everything about us has been borrowed. We have been lent by nature. It has given over to us parts of itself, thus precluding use for an infinite number of other things.

JEREMY RIFKIN

Life is partial, continuous, progressive, multiform and conditionally interactive, selfrealization of the potentialities of atomic electron states.

JOHN DESMOND BERNAL

Don't be angry with the rain; it simply does not know how to fall upward.

VLADIMIR NABOKOV

But I had a holy sense of a knowing universe, a universe unfolding, a universe of which we are privileged to be a part.

STUART KAUFFMAN

Two chemicals called actin and myosin evolved eons ago to allow the muscles in insect wings to contract and relax … Today, the same two proteins are responsible for the beating of the human heart.

DEEPAK CHOPRA

A pinhead heated to the temperature of the center of the Sun would emit enough heat to kill anyone who ventured within a thousand miles of it.

SIR JAMES JEANS

John Huston on seeing an old crone sitting on the curb in a town in Ireland, asked "What is life to you?" She, "A sigh between two mysteries."

Thank God stones are just stones, and rivers just rivers, and flowers just flowers.

FERNANDO PESSOA

Be earth now, and evensong. Be the ground lying under that sky. Be modest now, like a thing ripened until it is real, so that he who began it all can feel you when he reaches for you.

RAINER MARIA RILKE

LOVE LETTERS TO THE UNIVERSE

Breinigsville, PA USA
12 December 2010
251218BV00002B/5/P